UNSHAKEN

Faith-Filled Responses to Health Challenges

A Four-Week Devotional Bible Study by
Heather M. Dixon

Printed in the United States of America.
First Printing, 2024
ISBN-13: 9798329729351

To order additional copies of this resource, order online at www.amazon.com or visit www.therescuedletters.com for more information.

Cover Design: The Rescued Letters Collective

For
The Rescued Letters Collective Community
Because you
are one of the ways
God rescues me

CONTENTS

ABOUT THE AUTHOR

Heather M. Dixon is an author, speaker, Bible teacher, women's ministry coach and founder of The Rescued Letters Collective. Diagnosed with an incurable and terminal genetic disorder that she inherited from her mother, she is passionate about helping women find hope for their hard story by making the Bible available, relatable, and understandable. Heather serves as the Women's Ministry Director for her church in Raleigh and when she is not writing Bible studies or speaking at women's conferences and events, she loves to make the most of everyday moments such as cooking for her husband and son, checking out way too many library books, or unashamedly indulging in her love for all things Disney. Heather is a regular contributor to *Journey* magazine and the author of four Bible studies including *Determined: Living Like Jesus in Every Moment* and *Renewed: Finding Hope When You Don't Like Your Story*.

Connect with Heather:

Social Media: @rescuedletters
Podcast: *No Dusty Bibles* wherever you listen to podcasts
Website/Blog/Events + Booking Information: www.therescuedletters.com

INTRODUCTION

Welcome to *Unshaken: Faith-Filled Responses to Health Challenges*, a four-week devotional Bible study designed to help you explore the natural, human responses to health challenges alongside Scripture. When we experience a health challenge of any kind, whether it is our challenge or a challenge of someone that we love, it is normal and natural to respond with a wide variety of emotions and actions. This study is here to offer you solace and support, helping you to reclaim hope and peace in the midst of your challenge.

Here, we won't skip over or ignore those natural responses. Instead, we will journey through them with grace as we look to what the Bible has to say about each of these responses. Our ultimate goal is to allow the Word of God and His kindness to reframe our responses so that they are faith-filled and not fear-based.

Because I like to have an anchoring Scripture for any project, I have chosen a theme verse for this study—

Cast your burden on the LORD, and he will sustain you; he will never allow the righteous to be shaken.
Psalm 55:22 CSB

I encourage you to write this verse somewhere— on a note card, in your journal, on a sticky note, or in your smartphone. Write it somewhere so that you will see it everyday, remembering the truth of God's Word: that God will uphold you, keep you steady, and sustain you along every step of your health challenge. When our health, or the health of a loved one, is challenged, it is natural and normal to feel unsteady. It is normal to feel shaken in every way. But there is hope in God's Word and His compassionate love for us. You will get through this. You are not alone.

Over the next four weeks, we will explore the natural responses to health challenges, how to manage our fear and anxiety, and how to prioritize rest for ourselves even as we have concern for others in our life who are affected by our health challenge. We will consider how God's comfort and presence can sustain us, and how our own experiences with health challenges can equip us to comfort others. We will reflect on the bigger picture revealed in the truth of Scripture, that our challenges are never just about our individual story. Our health challenge is a part of a much greater story, one that can be used to bring much glory to God if we trust Him.

You are not alone on this path, and Jesus, the ultimate healer, is always close, ready to guide you towards a place of comfort, hope, and steadfastness. Each day offers a new opportunity to draw closer to Him and to find solace in His promises.

May God's comfort be tangibly near as you seek wisdom and peace from His Word.

A NOTE FROM HEATHER

I wish I could tell you that health challenges were not a part of my story. But you and I both know that the story of someone who never struggles with their health is like a unicorn: a beautiful ideal that doesn't exist. So let me tell you a bit about my story. After experiencing several back-to-back major medical events in the fall of 2015, I was diagnosed with Vascular Ehlers-Danlos Syndrome.

Vascular Ehlers-Danlos Syndrome (vEDS) is a genetic connective tissue disorder that makes organ and vascular tissue very fragile. The fragile portion of that definition means that for someone with vEDS (that's me!), blood vessels, arteries, and organs are prone to spontaneous rupture. The genetic portion of that definition means that it is usually inherited, and also that it is caused by a genetic mutation, specifically a mutation of the COL3A1 gene.

Here's a Quick Genetic Lesson from Someone Who Barely Remembers High School Biology:

Our DNA is made up of genes. And genes tell our bodies what to do and how to produce things that our bodies need. One of those things is protein. The body makes all different kinds of proteins. Collagen is one of the most abundant proteins in the body and the body makes all different types of collagen.

Collagen is like glue; it provides structure and holds the body together. Collagen is found in connective tissues. Connective tissues are called connective tissues for a reason. They keep stuff connected.

The COL3A1 gene instructs the body how to produce Type III Collagen, which is found in the skin, lungs, intestinal walls, and the walls of blood vessels and arteries. Since the COL3A1 gene is mutated for those with vEDS, Type III Collagen isn't made correctly. So for someone with vEDS, the connective tissues in the skin, lungs, intestines, blood vessels, and arteries are fragile. Hence the spontaneous rupture thing.

The COL3A1 gene can mutate in several different ways but ultimately that mutation means the body either doesn't produce enough collagen or it produces a normal amount of collagen, but it's all faulty. My specific mutation produces faulty collagen - every single collagen molecule in my body is wonky. So no, collagen supplements won't work on me but thanks for thinking of that.

What Happens to Someone with Vascular Ehlers-Danlos Syndrome?

Every vEDS patient experience is different, but the disorder manifests itself in similar ways. Those with vEDS often bruise easily and have thin, translucent skin with a lack of subcutaneous (that would be under the skin) tissue. Lobeless ears and hypermobility in small joints are common. And then there's the spontaneous rupture thing. This means expecting things like a perforated colon (yep, I've had that), aneurysms (got em), carotid artery dissection (check), miscarriage and pre-term labor caused by uterine rupture (check, check), collapsed lung (currently not on my medical chart), and aortic dissection (thankfully, not yet). Dissection is a fancy medical way of saying your arteries just cannot adult anymore and they promptly tear.

The life expectancy of someone with vEDS is usually cut short, with the average life expectancy around 50 years. Ongoing blood pressure management and quick triage by medical teams that know how to handle vEDS in the event of an acute emergency are key to survival.

Here's Why You Might Have Heard of Ehlers-Danlos Syndrome Before:

It's pretty rare, especially the vascular, and uh, rarer types. At the time of this printing, it is estimated that Vascular Ehlers-Danlos occurs in about 1 out of every 40,000-50,000 people.[1] Unfortunately, if someone has vEDS, it often isn't recognized until it takes their life. I am very fortunate to have a confirmed diagnosis.

Cures? Treatments? Isn't there something you can take?

Vascular Ehlers-Danlos is currently incurable and untreatable. However, I am thrilled to tell you that even since my diagnosis in 2016, there have been fantastic advancements in research for vEDS. There are doctors working to find a cure, or at least help to mitigate the risks associated with vEDS. But they are few and the resources they have to work with are fewer. In our modern world, where medicine is advancing faster than I can learn common core math, this is hard to accept. But this is the reality. I have been told by doctors to prepare my bucket list and live my life well.

Why am I telling you all this?

I am sharing this with you for two reasons.

One, because I want to help raise awareness and advocacy for vEDS. You've helped with that simply by purchasing this study. A portion of the proceeds from this study will go towards vEDS research. And that means that one day a young woman unknowingly carrying the vEDS genetic mutation won't have to sit in the emergency room for five hours in crippling pain as she loses a portion of her kidney tissue because the emergency staff assumed her pain was due to a stomach virus instead of a life-threatening renal dissection.*

I am also sharing this with you because I want you to know the words written in this study are brought to you from the trenches. Health challenges are a constant part of my story. Even four days into writing this study, I had to undergo a head and neck MRA scan and an emergency room visit for a vEDS complication that is still unresolved at the time of this printing. Indeed, I am walking through these pages right alongside you.

Here, I share the Bible passages, the stories, and the lessons that have brought me comfort through the darkest days. It is my deepest prayer they might be the catalyst that brings you hope and peace today.

I am rooting for you, always.

Heather

*Yes, this actually happened to me. May God richly bless the nurse who walked over and discreetly gave me pain medicine as I sat doubled over a chair in the emergency waiting room.

BEFORE WE BEGIN

It will benefit us both if I begin by telling you the things this study will not do.

This study will not give you medical advice. I am not a doctor. I have no special training in medicine, health care, psychology, or wellness. I am merely the survivor of an incurable genetic disorder that threatens major medical events. I've personally walked through the hard story of multiple health challenges. What follows in this study are all the human responses I have experienced with my own health challenges along with the Scriptures and truths from those Scriptures that have helped me respond in a more faithful way.

This study will not tell you all the things you are doing wrong so that you can then work harder to do them right. This is a come-as-you-are type of study. And I am a meet-you-where-you-are kind of teacher. I would never presume to know the journey you have taken to land here in these pages with me. And although I will always proclaim the blessings born from giving our time to worship God, pray to Him, and read His Word, I will not teach that you have to work harder to receive God's peace. The idea that one must work for God's grace is the antithesis of the gospel of Jesus Christ.

This study will not sugar coat the realities of broken bodies, nor will it delicately tap dance over the raw emotions that come when we face those realities. If you are wanting a study that sidesteps hard conversations and unspoken thoughts, this isn't for you. I share stories in these pages that may be graphic for some. I walk us through questions that typically float only in the backs of our minds. I confront issues that are admittedly difficult to process without a healthy toolkit of coping skills. At least, they have been for me.

So before we begin, I want to encourage you to seek support now in ways that will make you feel safe. God is certainly always with you, but His plan for the body of Christ is not that we should experience trials in isolation. He intends for Kingdom work to be done in the collective. This is hard work. And we need one another. Make sure you have someone you can call when the tears won't stop. Do identify now those who are in your inner circle and let them know what you are feeling. Don't be afraid to seek professional help; in fact, I highly encourage you to connect with a licensed mental health care provider to support you in this journey.

Finally, I want to remember our ultimate goal for our time together. In this study we want to take human responses to health challenges straight to the Word of God so that we can turn that response into a faith-filled response, one that will bring us the tangible gifts promised in God's Word. That when we cling to God, Jesus, and the Holy Spirit, we will receive the blessings of love, joy, peace, patience, kindness, goodness, faithfulness, gentleness, and self-control.[2] And ultimately our end goal is to place our lives in the loving hands of the Father who is always working for our good.

So join me in whispering this prayer before we begin: *Father, I want to trust you with this health challenge. Help me trust you more.*

WEEK ONE

Understanding Our Responses to Health Challenges

Ten visits to the emergency room. Nine surgeries. Major scans and imaging procedures? I can't even count the number. Let's just say I've been exposed to enough radiation to enable me to power a small city if I had to. I've driven down the road of health challenges several times. And with each challenge, I've noticed a pattern in how I respond.

It goes like this. First I ignore the problem.* It will go away if I just keep charging forward with the items on my to-do list. Ignore, distract, downplay. Can't hear out of my right ear? No worries, babe. It will clear up on it's own soon. Crippling stomach pain so bad I'm having trouble walking my son into daycare? Don't have time for that. I'm just gonna pull off on the side of the road to vomit and then I won't even be late for work.** I'm a professional at this first step. Please do not be like me.

Inevitably, the health challenge escalates which forces my hand to go see an actual doctor, request imaging procedures, or in many cases, visit the emergency room. Now armed with medical information that may or may not include an actual diagnosis, I have something tangible to ~~panic over~~ work with. We do, in fact, have an actual problem. I can no longer deny it, so I get mad at it. I am mad that I have to interrupt my beautiful life to address this health challenge. I am mad that my body isn't perfectly healthy like that cute girl with the perky ponytail who is always sharing her wellness routine on Instagram. (Her wellness routine is probably good genes. Let the reader understand.) Knowing that I live with a chronic illness, I am mad that my body has limitations and that I cannot run and go and do like normal people.*** I am MAD. I take angry walks. I play angry music. I silently scream into my pillow, but carefully so that I don't make my health challenge worse. And that just makes me more mad that I cannot scream like a normal person.*** I spend a considerable amount of time in this stage. Anger is easier than action.

Following my silent screams are my silent prayers. I start bargaining with God. See if these very real prayers of mine sound familiar to you: *Lord, if you'll just make it go away I promise I'll finally finish that writing project I've been working on for four years.**** Father, forgive me for not prioritizing my Scripture reading this morning. Look— I read three times more than my normal reading schedule today! I'll catch up I promise so can you fix this please? Jesus, I know my attitude has been poor lately. My eyes are open and I won't ever think that way again.* These examples are just a sampling of my response pattern in this stage. I beg and bargain with God to make it go away.

These are just some of the ways acute depression manifests during my health challenges. I should note here that even without health challenges, I have always been prone to depressive moods. The writer and creative in me simply cannot see only sunshine and rainbows in all things. Usually, all it takes is one song in a minor key and I enter the lamenting zone. But I digress; that's for another study. My point here is that I always travel through a depressive stage when processing a health challenge. But eventually, I do come to a place that resembles resolve.

I accept the health challenge. I wash my hands of the four previous stages I have walked through and I embrace the reality that on this side of heaven, I live in a broken body. And that means I will surely face health challenges until I meet Jesus face to face. And this acceptance ushers me into the courage required to take a step forward. I make the appointments with my doctor. I delve into books and journal articles that help me understand my health challenge better. I reach out to those who have walked through similar challenges to glean from their experience. *I move forward.*

As I think about these five different stages of my response to health challenges, I realize this pattern looks a lot like *the five stages of grief*. After observing the poor standard of treatment for terminal patients in hospitals, Dr. Elizabeth Kübler-Ross determined to sit with patients who were actively dying. Her goal was to listen to them, to give them space to process their emotions, and to honor their very sacred journey from life to death. Her observations during her time with these patients enabled her to draw conclusions that are commonly accepted today as the five stages of grief, which she explains in her 1969 bestselling book, *On Death and Dying*.[3]

The five stages of grief identified by Dr. Elizabeth Kübler-Ross are denial, anger, bargaining, depression, and acceptance. Although her conclusions stemmed from a very specific observational subset, terminal patients, I suspect you will agree with me that health challenges of any kind prompt a grief response. We grieve during health challenges because we experience loss. The loss of what used to be, the loss of stability in health, the loss of a future expectation from life, the loss of peace, joy, and contentment, and even sometimes the very dear loss of life itself.

It is natural and normal to experience a wide range of thoughts and feelings as you confront a health challenge. It is natural and normal to experience these thoughts and feelings even as a believer. I love Jesus with all my heart, mind, and soul but I need you to know that I do not automatically jump to *everything-is-going-to-be-okay* when I am dealing with a health crisis. It takes time, grace, and self-kindness to process scary realities when our health is threatened. The good news? God has all of those things, and more, in abundance.

God knows what keeps you up at night. He knows the prayers you don't have the courage to whisper. He knows the frailty of the human body as much as He knows your heart. And I can promise you this, He is kind and gracious and patient and loving and forgiving and compassionate enough to withstand all that you throw at Him.

So that is where I am asking you to start. 1 Peter 5:7 tells us to cast all our worries onto God because He cares for us. The word that Peter chooses for cast implies that we must hurl our worries at God.[4] It carries with it the imagery of someone lifting a giant boulder up and throwing it at someone with all their might. Why? Because God stands ready and willing to take it from you.

Over the next five days, we'll briefly walk through what the Bible says about denial, anger, bargaining, depression, and acceptance. We'll spend our time this week in the Psalms, because I like to think of it as a big book of feelings. The Psalms give words to emotions we cannot articulate and they help us communicate those feelings to God.

Let's hurl all of our feelings to God this week. He's ready.

This doesn't apply when the health challenge is a life-threatening issue, which I've experienced a number of times. In these situations, my response pattern goes straight to fear and anxiety, which we'll discuss next week.

**True story. My colon had perforated. Fun times.*

***There are no normal people.*

****Unleashed stans, it's coming I promise. Maybe.*

Week 1, Day 1: Oh, that I had wings like a dove

Today, we turn to Psalm 55, particularly focusing on verses 4-7, as we explore the theme of denial in the face of health challenges. This Psalm echoes the voice of someone overwhelmed by fear and wishing for escape, a feeling that might resonate with us when we face our own health crises. David, the author, vividly expresses his desire to flee from the turmoil that engulfs him, akin to our own wishes to escape the realities of illness or pain. As we read, let's reflect on how denial might initially serve as our instinctual shield against the harsh truths of our circumstances.

Psalm 55

1 Listen to my prayer, God.
Don't hide yourself from my supplication.
2 Attend to me, and answer me.
I am restless in my complaint,
and moan 3 because of the voice of the enemy,
because of the oppression of the wicked.
For they bring suffering on me.
In anger they hold a grudge against me.
4 My heart is severely pained within me.
The terrors of death have fallen on me.
5 Fearfulness and trembling have come on me.
Horror has overwhelmed me.
6 I said, "Oh that I had wings like a dove!
Then I would fly away, and be at rest.
7 Behold, then I would wander far off.
I would lodge in the wilderness."
Selah.

8 "I would hurry to a shelter from the stormy wind and storm."
9 Confuse them, Lord, and confound their language,
for I have seen violence and strife in the city.
10 Day and night they prowl around on its walls.
Malice and abuse are also within her.
11 Destructive forces are within her.
Threats and lies don't depart from her streets.
12 For it was not an enemy who insulted me,
then I could have endured it.
Neither was it he who hated me who raised himself up against me,
then I would have hidden myself from him.

13 But it was you, a man like me,
my companion, and my familiar friend.
14 We took sweet fellowship together.
We walked in God's house with company.
15 Let death come suddenly on them.
Let them go down alive into Sheol.*
For wickedness is among them, in their dwelling.
16 As for me, I will call on God.
The LORD will save me.
17 Evening, morning, and at noon, I will cry out in distress.
He will hear my voice.
18 He has redeemed my soul in peace from the battle that was against me,
although there are many who oppose me.
19 God, who is enthroned forever,
will hear and answer them.
Selah.

They never change
and don't fear God.
20 He raises his hands against his friends.
He has violated his covenant.
21 His mouth was smooth as butter,
but his heart was war.
His words were softer than oil,
yet they were drawn swords.

22 Cast your burden on the LORD and he will sustain you.
He will never allow the righteous to be moved.
23 But you, God, will bring them down into the pit of destruction.
Bloodthirsty and deceitful men shall not live out half their days,
but I will trust in you.

Journaling Questions

Spend a few moments today reflecting on the Scripture above, writing down any insights, questions, or prayers that come to mind. To get you started, I've given you a few questions to ponder below.

1. Verses 4-5 describe the feelings of distress and terror. Can you relate these emotions to a time when you first encountered or denied a health issue? How did you handle these overwhelming feelings?

2. David expresses a wish to fly away and find rest (v.6). When facing health challenges, have you ever wished to escape the reality of your situation? Describe that impulse and what prompts it.

3. David seeks a place of shelter to escape the stormy winds and tempest (v.8). What are your "shelters" or coping mechanisms when dealing with denial about your health? Are they helpful or do they hinder your acceptance and management of the situation?

4. Reflect on a time when denial might have delayed seeking help or treatment for a health issue. What were the consequences, and what have you learned from that experience?

5. Considering the weight of his troubles, David still calls out to God (v.16-17). How can you use your faith to move from denial to confronting and managing your health challenges more proactively?

_____

_____

_____

_____

_____

_____

_____

_____

_____

_____

_____

_____

_____

_____

_____

_____

_____

_____

Week 1, Day 2: Listen to the voice of my cry

On this second day, we delve into Psalm 5, where David communicates his feelings of frustration and implores God for justice against his enemies. This psalm can mirror the anger we might feel towards our own bodies or circumstances when faced with health challenges. David's candid approach in expressing his emotions towards God can guide us in acknowledging and channeling our own anger constructively. As we read, consider how David uses prayer not only to express his anger but also to seek guidance and assurance from God in the midst of his distress.

Psalm 5

1 Give ear to my words, LORD.
Consider my meditation.
2 Listen to the voice of my cry, my King and my God,
for I pray to you.
3 LORD, in the morning you will hear my voice.
In the morning I will lay my requests before you, and will watch expectantly.
4 For you are not a God who has pleasure in wickedness.
Evil can't live with you.
5 The arrogant will not stand in your sight.
You hate all workers of iniquity.
6 You will destroy those who speak lies.
The LORD abhors the bloodthirsty and deceitful man.
7 But as for me, in the abundance of your loving kindness I will come into your house.
I will bow toward your holy temple in reverence of you.
8 Lead me, LORD, in your righteousness because of my enemies.
Make your way straight before my face.
9 For there is no faithfulness in their mouth.
Their heart is destruction.
Their throat is an open tomb.
They flatter with their tongue.
10 Hold them guilty, God.
Let them fall by their own counsels.
Thrust them out in the multitude of their transgressions,
for they have rebelled against you.
11 But let all those who take refuge in you rejoice.
Let them always shout for joy, because you defend them.
Let them also who love your name be joyful in you.
12 For you will bless the righteous.
LORD, you will surround him with favor as with a shield.

Journaling Questions

Spend a few moments today reflecting on the Scripture above, writing down any insights, questions, or prayers that come to mind.

1. David begins his prayer by asking God to consider his words and listen to his cry for help (v.1-2). When you are angry about your health situation, how do you express it to God? Do you feel comfortable sharing your true feelings with Him?

2. In verse 3, David mentions that he lays his requests before God in the morning. How can establishing a routine of laying out your frustrations and requests each morning affect your handling of anger related to health challenges?

3. Reflect on a time when anger about your health led to negative consequences either for yourself or others around you. What might you have learned from that situation about managing anger more healthily?

4. David trusts that God will lead him in righteousness despite his enemies (v.8). How can focusing on God's righteousness and guidance help you deal with anger concerning ongoing health issues?

5. Consider David's plea for protection from those who do evil (v.11-12). How can you apply this plea to seek protection from the destructive aspects of anger in your own life while navigating health challenges?

_____

_____

_____

_____

_____

_____

_____

_____

_____

_____

_____

Week 1, Day 3: Lord, be my helper

As we explore the theme of bargaining in our journey through health challenges, Psalm 30 offers profound insights into the dynamics of pleading and negotiating with God during times of distress. In this Psalm, David celebrates his deliverance from near-death experiences, acknowledging the mercy of God in rescuing him from the depths. His expressions of gratitude mixed with previous desperate pleas provide a powerful backdrop for understanding how we might also bargain with God in our times of health crises. Let this Psalm guide us in reflecting on the nature of our bargains with God and the deeper trust that can emerge from these conversations.

Psalm 30

1 I will extol you, LORD, for you have raised me up,
and have not made my foes to rejoice over me.
2 LORD my God, I cried to you,
and you have healed me.
3 LORD, you have brought up my soul from Sheol.*
You have kept me alive, that I should not go down to the pit.
4 Sing praise to the LORD, you saints of his.
Give thanks to his holy name.
5 For his anger is but for a moment.
His favor is for a lifetime.
Weeping may stay for the night,
but joy comes in the morning.
6 As for me, I said in my prosperity,
"I shall never be moved."
7 You, LORD, when you favored me, made my mountain stand strong;
but when you hid your face, I was troubled.
8 I cried to you, LORD.
I made supplication to the Lord:
9 "What profit is there in my destruction, if I go down to the pit?
Shall the dust praise you?
Shall it declare your truth?
10 Hear, LORD, and have mercy on me.
LORD, be my helper."
11 You have turned my mourning into dancing for me.
You have removed my sackcloth, and clothed me with gladness,
12 to the end that my heart may sing praise to you, and not be silent.
LORD my God, I will give thanks to you forever!

Journaling Questions

Spend a few moments today reflecting on the Scripture above, writing down any insights, questions, or prayers that come to mind.

1. David speaks of crying out to God for help and receiving healing (v.2). Think of a time when you bargained with God during a health crisis. What did you promise or ask for, and how did you feel about this exchange?

2. Consider the phrase, "To you, O Lord, I called; to the Lord I cried for mercy" (v.8). How do you reconcile the act of bargaining with a sincere faith in God's plan for your health and life?

3. In verse 9, David questions what benefit there is in his demise, appealing to God's desire for praise and thanksgiving. Have you ever used similar logic in your prayers during difficult health situations? Reflect on the implications of this kind of bargaining.

4. David shifts from mourning to dancing, from sackcloth to joy (v.11-12). How does this transformation reflect the potential outcomes of our own bargaining with God? Have there been instances where your bargaining led to a deeper understanding or change in perspective?

5. Psalm 30 ends with praise and thanksgiving for God's favor (v.12). How can you move from bargaining to gratitude in your own health journey, regardless of the outcome?

Week 1, Day 4: Be to me a strong rock

Today, we reflect on Psalm 31, a poignant scripture that resonates deeply when we grapple with depression amidst health challenges. David's heartfelt plea for deliverance and his lament about being a "broken vessel" vividly capture the essence of feeling forsaken and overwhelmed by life's trials. As we navigate through his words, we see a powerful expression of despair mixed with steadfast trust in God's deliverance. This psalm can help us articulate our own feelings of depression and guide us in seeking God's presence and relief during our darkest times.

Psalm 31

1 In you, LORD, I take refuge.
Let me never be disappointed.
Deliver me in your righteousness.
2 Bow down your ear to me.
Deliver me speedily.
Be to me a strong rock,
a house of defense to save me.
3 For you are my rock and my fortress,
therefore for your name's sake lead me and guide me.
4 Pluck me out of the net that they have laid secretly for me,
for you are my stronghold.
5 Into your hand I commend my spirit.
You redeem me, LORD, God of truth.
6 I hate those who regard lying vanities,
but I trust in the LORD.
7 I will be glad and rejoice in your loving kindness,
for you have seen my affliction.
You have known my soul in adversities.
8 You have not shut me up into the hand of the enemy.
You have set my feet in a large place.
9 Have mercy on me, LORD, for I am in distress.
My eye, my soul, and my body waste away with grief.
10 For my life is spent with sorrow,
my years with sighing.
My strength fails because of my iniquity.
My bones are wasted away.
11 Because of all my adversaries I have become utterly contemptible to my neighbors,
a horror to my acquaintances.
Those who saw me on the street fled from me.
12 I am forgotten from their hearts like a dead man.
I am like broken pottery.

13 For I have heard the slander of many, terror on every side,
while they conspire together against me,
they plot to take away my life.
14 But I trust in you, LORD.
I said, "You are my God."
15 My times are in your hand.
Deliver me from the hand of my enemies, and from those who persecute me.
16 Make your face to shine on your servant.
Save me in your loving kindness.
17 Let me not be disappointed, LORD, for I have called on you.
Let the wicked be disappointed.
Let them be silent in Sheol.*
18 Let the lying lips be mute,
which speak against the righteous insolently, with pride and contempt.
19 Oh how great is your goodness,
which you have laid up for those who fear you,
which you have worked for those who take refuge in you,
before the sons of men!
20 In the shelter of your presence you will hide them from the plotting of man.
You will keep them secretly in a dwelling away from the strife of tongues.
21 Praise be to the LORD,
for he has shown me his marvelous loving kindness in a strong city.
22 As for me, I said in my haste, "I am cut off from before your eyes."
Nevertheless you heard the voice of my petitions when I cried to you.
23 Oh love the LORD, all you his saints!
The LORD preserves the faithful,
and fully recompenses him who behaves arrogantly.
24 Be strong, and let your heart take courage,
all you who hope in the LORD.

Journaling Questions

Spend a few moments today reflecting on the Scripture above, writing down any insights, questions, or prayers that come to mind.

1. David describes his distress and sorrow, his body and soul consumed by grief (v.9-10). How does this reflection of deep despair resonate with your own experiences during health challenges? Can you identify a time when you felt similarly overwhelmed?

2. David feels forgotten and discarded, like a broken vessel (v.12). Have there been moments in your health journey when you've felt broken or forgotten? How did you address these feelings with God or others?

3. In verse 14, despite his anguish, David asserts, "But I trust in you, LORD; I say, 'You are my God.'" How can declaring your trust in God, even in the midst of depression, alter your emotional or spiritual state?

4. At the end of the psalm, David praises God for his goodness (v.19-21). How can focusing on the goodness of God, even when it feels distant, provide a counterbalance to the weight of depression in your life?

5. Reflect on the way David handles his emotions by being brutally honest in his prayer (v.22). How does expressing your true feelings to God during depression help you in coping with these intense emotions?

_____

_____

_____

_____

_____

_____

_____

_____

_____

_____

_____

_____

_____

_____

_____

_____

_____

_____

Week 1, Day 5: Be still and know

On this final day of our first week, we delve into Psalm 46, a powerful declaration of God's presence and strength in tumultuous times. This psalm is a beacon of hope and a foundation for acceptance, asserting God as our refuge and strength, an ever-present help in trouble. As we face health challenges, embracing acceptance doesn't mean giving up; it means acknowledging our reality and trusting in God's unwavering support. Let's explore how this acknowledgment can lead to a profound sense of peace and resilience, even amidst life's storms.

Psalm 46

1 God is our refuge and strength,
a very present help in trouble.
2 Therefore we won't be afraid, though the earth changes,
though the mountains are shaken into the heart of the seas;
3 though its waters roar and are troubled,
though the mountains tremble with their swelling.
Selah.

4 There is a river, the streams of which make the city of God glad,
the holy place of the tents of the Most High.
5 God is within her. She shall not be moved.
God will help her at dawn.
6 The nations raged. The kingdoms were moved.
He lifted his voice and the earth melted.
7 The LORD of Armies is with us.
The God of Jacob is our refuge.
Selah.

8 Come, see the LORD's works,
what desolations he has made in the earth.
9 He makes wars cease to the end of the earth.
He breaks the bow, and shatters the spear.
He burns the chariots in the fire.
10 "Be still, and know that I am God.
I will be exalted among the nations.
I will be exalted in the earth."
11 The LORD of Armies is with us.
The God of Jacob is our refuge.

Journaling Questions

Spend a few moments today reflecting on the Scripture above, writing down any insights, questions, or prayers that come to mind.

1. "God is our refuge and strength, an ever-present help in trouble" (v.1). How does recognizing God as your refuge change your approach to accepting health challenges?

2. The psalmist describes a world in chaos, where mountains fall and waters roar (v.2-3). Can you relate these images to the turmoil you've felt with your health issues? How does framing your situation within this context of natural upheaval help in moving toward acceptance?

3. The City of God is described as unshakable because God is within her (v.5). How can you cultivate a similar unshakable spirit within yourself by accepting God's presence in your life, especially during health challenges?

4. "Be still, and know that I am God" (v.10). What are some ways you can practice being still in the midst of your health struggles? How might stillness lead to deeper acceptance?

5. Reflect on how the themes of this psalm—God's power and protection—can guide you from struggling against your reality to embracing it with faith and trust. How does acceptance of your circumstances enable you to experience God's peace more fully?

_____

_____

_____

_____

_____

_____

_____

_____

_____

_____

_____

_____

_____

_____

Week 1 Wrap-Up

As we conclude the first week of our journey through *Unshaken: Faith-Filled Responses to Health Challenges*, it's important to reflect on the profound insights and emotional experiences we've encountered. This week, we've explored the theme of understanding our responses to health challenges through the lens of the five stages of grief: denial, anger, bargaining, depression, and acceptance. Each day, we've delved into scriptures that help articulate these feelings, offering us God's perspective on handling such emotions.

At the end of every week, I will offer a list of practical tools to assist you at each step. Read through them, and perhaps circle the tools that might be a good fit for you. This list is not exhaustive, and as you find other tools that work for you, jot them down at the end of every week so you can build your personalized resource section.

Practical Tools for Navigating Natural Responses

Recognize and Label Emotions:

Tool: Journaling. Maintain a daily journal where you not only record your thoughts and emotions but also label them. This practice can help you identify patterns in your emotional responses and better understand how they influence your handling of health challenges.

Addressing Denial:

Tool: Accountability. Share your health status and feelings with a trusted friend, family member, or support group regularly. This can help prevent you from ignoring symptoms or emotions that need attention.

Managing Anger:

Tool: Physical Activity. Engage in moderate exercise, like walking or stretching, which can serve as a healthy outlet for frustration and anger. Additionally, consider activities that prioritize serenity, like painting or gardening, to help soothe angry emotions.

Coping with Bargaining:

Tool: Prayer and Scripture Meditation. Structure your prayer time to not only make requests but also to meditate on scriptures that reinforce God's sovereignty and goodness. This can help shift your focus from bargaining to trusting in God's plan.

Dealing with Depression:

Tool: Professional Support. If depression becomes overwhelming, seeking help from a mental health professional can be crucial. Also, engage in community activities that uplift your spirit and keep you connected to others.

Embracing Acceptance

Tool: Education and Advocacy. Learn as much as you can about your health condition and become an advocate for your own care. Encouragement through knowledge can help you accept your health challenges and actively participate in decision-making regarding treatments and management.

Routine Creation:

Tool: Establish a daily routine that includes dedicated time for spiritual practices, self-care, and rest. A consistent routine can help manage the unpredictability of health challenges and provide a sense of control and normalcy.

Enhance Communication with Health Providers:

Tool: Informed Discussions. Keep a detailed health diary that includes symptoms, medication effects, dietary habits, and emotional states. This record can be invaluable during appointments with your healthcare providers, ensuring that your discussions are informed and productive.

Cultivating Community Support:

Tool: Support Groups. Participate in or start a support group specific to your health condition. Sharing experiences and solutions with others who understand can be incredibly comforting and informative.

Spiritual Reinforcement:

Tool: Scripture Memorization. Memorize scriptures that speak to each stage of your emotional response to health challenges. These verses can serve as quick reminders of God's presence and promises when you feel overwhelmed.

Reflection

This week's journey has highlighted that our initial emotional responses to health challenges are natural and expected. By acknowledging these responses and equipping ourselves with practical tools to manage them, we move towards a more faith-filled approach to our trials. Each stage of grief, when navigated thoughtfully and prayerfully, can lead us closer to understanding ourselves and deepening our reliance on God.

As you continue to reflect on this week's lessons, remember that each step forward, no matter how small, is significant. Our responses to health challenges are not linear; they ebb and flow as circumstances change. However, the tools we've discussed can provide a foundation for handling these changes with grace and faith.

Prayer for the Week

Heavenly Father, thank You for Your presence this week as we navigated through the complex emotions of dealing with health challenges. We ask for Your guidance in applying the tools we've learned, to not only manage our responses but to transform them into expressions of faith and trust in You. Help us to remember that You are with us in every moment, ready to provide strength, comfort, and peace. In Jesus' name, Amen.

As we move forward into the next week, let's carry with us the lessons of acceptance and the readiness to apply the tools we've gathered, knowing that through God, we can face each day with courage and hope.

WEEK TWO

Managing Fear & Anxiety

It is natural to experience fear and anxiety in a health challenge. It is natural to experience fear and anxiety in a health challenge. It is natural to experience fear and anxiety in a health challenge.

You are not alone. You are not alone. You are not alone.

Yes, the repetition of both of those sentences is intentional. Why? Because they are worth repeating, especially for those of us in a faith community. Let me share something I've observed. Most humans are uncomfortable with the raw expression of pain, grief, sorrow, fear, and anxiety. That's understandable. No one wants to get cozy with hard things. We want the easy button. We want the fast pass. We want the exit ramp to relief.

So when our health challenge prompts a response of fear or anxiety, I've observed that we tend to brush that response off quickly. *I'm fine. Everything's okay. Nothing to worry about, nothing to see here.* Perhaps we embrace these superficial responses because it's easier— not just for us but also because we want to protect those who express concern for us in a health challenge.

Meanwhile, our minds are racing with a million *what-if's,* our belly is burning with dread, our breath is shallow, we can't focus, our nights are restless, and we awake to an overall feeling of unease that never really goes away. This is how fear and anxiety show up in my life. I bet you can relate. I bet you can add a few of your own examples.

Health challenges produce some of my scariest bouts with anxiety. And what I dearly want you to know today is that your struggle with anxiety is not a faltering in your faith. You don't love Jesus less because you worry about tomorrow. Needing support for your journey with anxiety doesn't make you less of a Christian. Jesus isn't disappointed in your panic attack.

If you struggle with fear and anxiety during a health challenge, I wish I could have you over for coffee. I put whipped cream in my coffee every morning; how do you like yours? We'd sit on my back porch, listen to the birds sing, and feel the breeze roll through as we shared hard moments and encouraging hugs. My backyard birds are the best, by the way. They are guaranteed to make you smile.

But since I can't have you over for coffee, I hope what I share here will encourage you today:

You are not alone in your struggle. One of the greatest lies we can tell ourselves is that we are alone in our suffering. And it's just exactly that: a lie. I dare you to look a stranger in the eye today. Given that nineteen percent of Americans suffer from anxiety, chances are good you won't have to look too many strangers in the eye before you are met with an anxious stare.[5]

But I'd also tell you that your fellow humans aren't the only ones who understand what you are going through. Read Luke's words describing Jesus' experience as He anticipated the cross:

He was withdrawn from them about a stone's throw, and he knelt down and prayed, saying, "Father, if you are willing, remove this cup from me. Nevertheless, not my will, but yours, be done." An angel from heaven appeared to him, strengthening him. Being in agony, he prayed more earnestly. His sweat became like great drops of blood falling down on the ground.

Luke 22:41-44

The word used to describe Jesus' emotions as he prepared to face the cross is agony. The Greek transliteration used here for agony is *agonia*, which means – great fear, terror, of death; anxiety, agony.

Jesus understands anxiety. He knows what it's like to feel the heart pounding between uneven and shallow breaths. He even knows what it feels like to sweat blood. Not once does He hear your prayer for relief and respond with trite and pithy instructions to "shake it off" or "get over it". When you think that no one around you understands, remember that your Savior does because He's lived it in the flesh.

Start small. Anxiety operates like a snowball rolling from the top of a giant mountain until it completely runs you over as you stand near the bottom. At least, that's what it feels like for me. It will start small and eventually build into something that feels unmanageable. Take baby steps. Build your toolbox for battling anxiety (spoiler alert: more tips for that are in this week's wrap-up) and address one item in it at a time. Don't overwhelm yourself with a complete overhaul because that might lead to more anxiety.

Build your anxiety-battling toolbox. I'm a big believer in toolboxes. All of our efforts must start with God's Word, but we need practical tools and strategies to support what it says if we want to move forward. Enter the anxiety-battling toolbox. These are actions and items that help you in the moment, in the baby steps, and through to the other side of relief. Here's a glance at mine:

Intimacy with the Lord – Prayer, the Study of God's Word, and Worship

This has to come first. We cannot expect to receive heavenly comfort if we are not comfortable in the Lord's presence. My most profound moments of relief from anxiety always come in times of earnest and heartfelt prayer, Bible study, and worship. These aren't obligations to the Christian faith, these are mechanisms of blessing.

Community – Time with Family, Friends, and the Church Body

Being a part of a community is an in-your-face reminder that you are not alone. Fellowship and community is God's design for us. Your family, your friends, your church body – spend dedicated time with them. Eat together. Laugh together. Make memories together. Share prayer requests with one another. Lift one another up and encourage one another.

Nourish Your Soul – Spend Time Doing What You Love

This one will look differently for everyone because we are not all wired the same way. What feeds my soul might not feed yours. For me, this includes time alone (introverts, unite!), reading, getting outside, and creating something new. Put taking care of yourself near the top of your to-do list.

Start with intimacy with the Lord (you're doing that right here in this study, high-fives!) and then build your toolbox one step at a time and know that the rest will be there when you are ready for it. As you begin to feel comfortable with the whole of your toolbox, train yourself to look for balance. When pieces of my toolbox are overly neglected, my anxiety escalates.

One final note before we move on to our Scriptures for this week. I often wish that God would outright remove my sensitivity to anxiety. I do wish that He would take it away and I ask Him for that because I know He absolutely can. And sometimes, He does. But most of the time, I find that health-related anxiety is an opportunity for me to trust Him more. Anxiety is a burden that keeps me tethered to Him.

And that's a beautiful place to reside.

Week 2, Day 1: I will fear no evil

As we embark on Week 2 of our journey in *Unshaken: Faith-Filled Responses to Health Challenges*, we start by addressing the human emotion of fear through the comforting words of Psalm 23. This beloved psalm, often recited in times of distress, serves as a profound reminder of God's presence and protection. David, the shepherd king, eloquently describes God as a shepherd who guides and cares for His flock, ensuring they lack nothing, even in the darkest valleys. As we delve into this scripture, let's explore how understanding and trusting in God's guidance can alleviate our fears, especially those stirred by health challenges.

Psalm 23

1 The LORD is my shepherd;
I shall lack nothing.
2 He makes me lie down in green pastures.
He leads me beside still waters.
3 He restores my soul.
He guides me in the paths of righteousness for his name's sake.
4 Even though I walk through the valley of the shadow of death,
I will fear no evil, for you are with me.
Your rod and your staff,
they comfort me.
5 You prepare a table before me
in the presence of my enemies.
You anoint my head with oil.
My cup runs over.
6 Surely goodness and loving kindness shall follow me all the days of my life,
and I will dwell in the LORD's house forever.

Journaling Questions

Spend a few moments today reflecting on the Scripture above, writing down any insights, questions, or prayers that come to mind.

1. "The Lord is my shepherd; I shall not want" (v.1). Reflect on how recognizing God as your shepherd can influence your perception of fear. How does this image comfort you in times when health worries loom large?

2. "He leads me beside still waters. He restores my soul" (v.2-3). Consider a time when fear due to a health issue felt overwhelming. How can the idea of God leading you to 'still waters' and restoring your soul guide your response to such fears?

3. "Even though I walk through the darkest valley, I will fear no evil, for you are with me" (v.4). What does it mean to you to walk through a 'darkest valley' in terms of health challenges? How does the assurance that God is with you change your experience of this journey?

4. "Your rod and your staff, they comfort me" (v.4). Rods and staffs are tools shepherds use to guide and protect sheep. How can you apply the concept of God's 'rod and staff' in managing your fears about health?

5. Reflect on the promise of dwelling in the house of the Lord forever (v.6). How does focusing on this eternal perspective help manage immediate fears related to your health? How might this assurance affect your day-to-day life?

_____

_____

_____

_____

_____

_____

_____

_____

_____

_____

_____

_____

_____

_____

_____

_____

_____

_____

Week 2, Day 2: Be strong and courageous

Today, we explore the potent theme of managing fear through the powerful words spoken to Joshua, particularly in Joshua 1:6-9. As Joshua prepares to lead the Israelites into the Promised Land, God commands him to be strong and courageous, not once but multiple times, emphasizing the need for courage in the face of daunting challenges. This passage not only highlights the importance of divine encouragement but also offers us a blueprint for confronting our own fears, especially when navigating health challenges. Let's reflect on how God's command to Joshua can be applied to our lives, providing us with the strength to manage fear with faith.

Joshua 1

Now after the death of Moses the servant of the LORD,* the LORD spoke to Joshua the son of Nun, Moses' servant, saying, 2 "Moses my servant is dead. Now therefore arise, go across this Jordan, you and all these people, to the land which I am giving to them, even to the children of Israel. 3 I have given you every place that the sole of your foot will tread on, as I told Moses. 4 From the wilderness and this Lebanon even to the great river, the river Euphrates, all the land of the Hittites, and to the great sea toward the going down of the sun, shall be your border. 5 No man will be able to stand before you all the days of your life. As I was with Moses, so I will be with you. I will not fail you nor forsake you.

6 "Be strong and courageous; for you shall cause this people to inherit the land which I swore to their fathers to give them. 7 Only be strong and very courageous. Be careful to observe to do according to all the law which Moses my servant commanded you. Don't turn from it to the right hand or to the left, that you may have good success wherever you go. 8 This book of the law shall not depart from your mouth, but you shall meditate on it day and night, that you may observe to do according to all that is written in it; for then you shall make your way prosperous, and then you shall have good success. 9 Haven't I commanded you? Be strong and courageous. Don't be afraid. Don't be dismayed, for the LORD your God† is with you wherever you go."

10 Then Joshua commanded the officers of the people, saying, 11 "Pass through the middle of the camp, and command the people, saying, 'Prepare food; for within three days you are to pass over this Jordan, to go in to possess the land which the LORD your God gives you to possess.' "

12 Joshua spoke to the Reubenites, and to the Gadites, and to the half-tribe of Manasseh, saying, 13 "Remember the word which Moses the servant of the LORD commanded you, saying, 'The LORD your God gives you rest, and will give you this land. 14 Your wives, your little ones, and your livestock shall live in the land which Moses gave you beyond the Jordan; but you shall pass over before your brothers armed, all the mighty men of valor, and shall help them 15 until the LORD has given your brothers rest, as he has given you, and they have also possessed the land which the LORD your God gives them. Then you shall return to the land of your possession and possess it, which Moses the servant of the LORD gave you beyond the Jordan toward the sunrise.' "

16 They answered Joshua, saying, "All that you have commanded us we will do, and wherever you send us we will go. 17 Just as we listened to Moses in all things, so will we listen to you. Only may the LORD your God be with you, as he was with Moses. 18 Whoever rebels against your commandment, and doesn't listen to your words in all that you command him shall himself be put to death. Only be strong and courageous."

Journaling Questions

Spend a few moments today reflecting on the Scripture above, writing down any insights, questions, or prayers that come to mind.

1. "Be strong and courageous" (v.6, 7, 9). How does repeating this command from God impact your feelings when you face fear regarding your health? How can you apply this divine encouragement to specific fears you are currently facing?

2. Consider the role of God's law in Joshua's courage (v.7-8). How can staying immersed in Scripture and God's promises serve as a tool to manage your fears? Can you think of other verses that reinforce this message of courage?

3. God promises Joshua that He will never leave nor forsake him (v.9). How does knowing that God is always with you change your approach to dealing with fears about your health?

4. "Do not be terrified; do not be discouraged" (v.9). What practical steps can you take to heed this advice in your everyday life, especially when fears about health arise unexpectedly?

5. Reflect on a past situation where you felt overwhelmed by fear due to a health issue. How did you handle it, and how might applying the lessons from Joshua 1:6-9 change your response if faced with a similar situation in the future?

_____

_____

_____

_____

_____

_____

_____

_____

_____

_____

Week 2, Day 3: You perceive my thoughts from afar

On this third day of our second week focusing on managing fear and anxiety, we turn to Psalm 139, a profound meditation on God's intimate knowledge and constant presence in our lives. This psalm provides a comforting reassurance that we are never alone or unseen, even in our most anxious moments. David's words illustrate a deep sense of security derived from the understanding that God has searched us thoroughly and knows us completely—our thoughts, our paths, and our lying down are all familiar to Him. As we reflect on this psalm, consider how the recognition of God's omnipresence can alleviate the anxieties associated with health challenges.

Psalm 139

1 LORD, you have searched me,
and you know me.
2 You know my sitting down and my rising up.
You perceive my thoughts from afar.
3 You search out my path and my lying down,
and are acquainted with all my ways.
4 For there is not a word on my tongue,
but behold, LORD, you know it altogether.
5 You hem me in behind and before.
You laid your hand on me.
6 This knowledge is beyond me.
It's lofty.
I can't attain it.
7 Where could I go from your Spirit?
Or where could I flee from your presence?
8 If I ascend up into heaven, you are there.
If I make my bed in Sheol,* behold, you are there!
9 If I take the wings of the dawn,
and settle in the uttermost parts of the sea,
10 even there your hand will lead me,
and your right hand will hold me.
11 If I say, "Surely the darkness will overwhelm me.
The light around me will be night,"
12 even the darkness doesn't hide from you,
but the night shines as the day.
The darkness is like light to you.

13 For you formed my inmost being.
You knit me together in my mother's womb.
14 I will give thanks to you,
for I am fearfully and wonderfully made.
Your works are wonderful.
My soul knows that very well.
15 My frame wasn't hidden from you,
when I was made in secret,
woven together in the depths of the earth.
16 Your eyes saw my body.
In your book they were all written,
the days that were ordained for me,
when as yet there were none of them.
17 How precious to me are your thoughts, God!
How vast is their sum!
18 If I would count them, they are more in number than the sand.
When I wake up, I am still with you.
19 If only you, God, would kill the wicked.
Get away from me, you bloodthirsty men!
20 For they speak against you wickedly.
Your enemies take your name in vain.
21 LORD, don't I hate those who hate you?
Am I not grieved with those who rise up against you?
22 I hate them with perfect hatred.
They have become my enemies.
23 Search me, God, and know my heart.
Try me, and know my thoughts.
24 See if there is any wicked way in me,
and lead me in the everlasting way.

Journaling Questions

Spend a few moments today reflecting on the Scripture above, writing down any insights, questions, or prayers that come to mind.

1. "You have searched me, Lord, and you know me" (v.1). How does knowing that God understands your deepest fears and anxieties change your emotional response when dealing with health challenges?

2. "Where can I go from your Spirit? Where can I flee from your presence?" (v.7). Reflect on a time when you felt isolated by anxiety. How does this passage comfort you in knowing that God's presence encompasses all places and situations?

3. "You knit me together in my mother's womb... I am fearfully and wonderfully made" (v.13-14). How can meditating on the fact that God intricately created you help manage anxiety about your health or physical limitations?

4. "Search me, God, and know my heart; test me and know my anxious thoughts" (v.23-24). What specific anxieties have you experienced regarding your health? How can inviting God to search and know these fears lead to peace and reassurance?

5. Consider how the themes of being known and loved by God could transform your approach to anxiety. How can embracing these truths encourage you to hand over your anxieties to God more freely?

_____

_____

_____

_____

_____

_____

_____

_____

_____

_____

_____

_____

_____

_____

_____

_____

_____

_____

Week 2, Day 4: The God of peace will be with you

Today, we engage with Philippians 4:4-9, a passage that provides clear directives on managing anxiety through rejoicing, prayer, and reflective thinking. Paul, writing from a place of confinement, teaches us how to find peace that transcends understanding by focusing on what is true, noble, right, pure, lovely, and admirable. As we read this encouraging text, let's consider how these instructions can be applied to our struggles with anxiety, particularly in the context of health challenges, guiding us towards a peaceful and trusting mindset in God.

Philippians 4:4-9

Rejoice in the Lord always! Again I will say, "Rejoice!" 5 Let your gentleness be known to all men. The Lord is at hand. 6 In nothing be anxious, but in everything, by prayer and petition with thanksgiving, let your requests be made known to God. 7 And the peace of God, which surpasses all understanding,
will guard your hearts and your thoughts in Christ Jesus.

8 Finally, brothers, whatever things are true, whatever things are honorable, whatever things are just, whatever things are pure, whatever things are lovely, whatever things are of good report: if there is any virtue and if there is anything worthy of praise, think about these things. 9 Do the things which you learned, received, heard, and saw in me, and the God of peace will be with you.

Journaling Questions

Spend a few moments today reflecting on the Scripture above, writing down any insights, questions, or prayers that come to mind.

1. "Rejoice in the Lord always. I will say it again: Rejoice!" (v.4). How can maintaining a spirit of joy, even in difficult times, impact your anxiety levels? What are practical ways you can cultivate joy in your daily life despite health challenges?

2. "Do not be anxious about anything, but in every situation, by prayer and petition, with thanksgiving, present your requests to God" (v.6). Reflect on how changing your prayer life to include thanksgiving can alter your experience of anxiety. Can you think of a recent situation where you could have applied this advice?

3. "The peace of God, which transcends all understanding, will guard your hearts and your minds in Christ Jesus" (v.7). What does it mean to you that God's peace can guard your heart and mind? How can you more fully allow this peace to influence your thoughts and feelings about health issues?

4. Paul advises focusing on things that are true, noble, right, pure, lovely, and admirable (v.8). List some aspects of your life and your surroundings that fit these descriptions. How can intentionally focusing on these positive elements help manage anxiety?

5. Consider the promise that the God of peace will be with you (v.9). How does this assurance affect your view of managing anxiety? Discuss a time when you felt God's peace during a particularly anxious period related to your health.

_____

_____

_____

_____

_____

_____

_____

_____

_____

_____

_____

_____

_____

_____

_____

_____

_____

_____

_____

Week 2, Day 5: Consider the lilies

On the final day of this week's focus on managing fear and anxiety, we turn to Matthew 6:25-34, where Jesus addresses the futility of worry and the importance of trusting in God's provision. This passage invites us to stay grounded in the present, teaching us to not be consumed by anxieties about the future, particularly those related to our health. Jesus emphasizes the care that God shows even to the smallest parts of creation, reassuring us of how much more He cares for us. As we read these verses, let's reflect on how this message can help us shift our focus from anxious thoughts about what might happen to a peaceful acceptance of God's grace in the current moment.

Matthew 6:25-34

Therefore I tell you, don't be anxious for your life: what you will eat, or what you will drink; nor yet for your body, what you will wear. Isn't life more than food, and the body more than clothing? 26 See the birds of the sky, that they don't sow, neither do they reap, nor gather into barns. Your heavenly Father feeds them. Aren't you of much more value than they?

27 "Which of you by being anxious, can add one moment‡ to his lifespan? 28 Why are you anxious about clothing? Consider the lilies of the field, how they grow. They don't toil, neither do they spin, 29 yet I tell you that even Solomon in all his glory was not dressed like one of these. 30 But if God so clothes the grass of the field, which today exists and tomorrow is thrown into the oven, won't he much more clothe you, you of little faith?

31 "Therefore don't be anxious, saying, 'What will we eat?', 'What will we drink?' or, 'With what will we be clothed?' 32 For the Gentiles seek after all these things; for your heavenly Father knows that you need all these things. 33 But seek first God's Kingdom and his righteousness; and all these things will be given to you as well. 34 Therefore don't be anxious for tomorrow, for tomorrow will be anxious for itself. Each day's own evil is sufficient.

Journaling Questions

Spend a few moments today reflecting on the Scripture above, writing down any insights, questions, or prayers that come to mind.

1. "Therefore I tell you, do not worry about your life, what you will eat or drink; or about your body, what you will wear" (v.25). How can Jesus' directive to not worry about life's basic needs be applied to anxieties you have about health challenges?

2. "Look at the birds of the air; they do not sow or reap or store away in barns, and yet your heavenly Father feeds them. Are you not much more valuable than they?" (v.26). How does this comparison enhance your understanding of God's care for you, especially in times of health-related anxiety?

3. "Can any one of you by worrying add a single hour to your life?" (v.27). Reflect on the practicality of this question. How has worry impacted your health or wellbeing negatively, and what steps can you take to mitigate this?

4. Consider the admonition to seek first God's kingdom and His righteousness (v.33). How can prioritizing spiritual growth and reliance on God reduce anxieties about health and lead to a more grounded life?

5. "So do not worry about tomorrow, for tomorrow will worry about itself. Each day has enough trouble of its own" (v.34). Discuss the benefits of focusing on the present rather than anxieties about the future. How can staying present help you manage health-related fears more effectively?

_____

_____

_____

_____

_____

_____

_____

_____

_____

_____

_____

_____

_____

_____

_____

_____

_____

_____

Week 2 Wrap-Up

As we conclude our second week of *Unshaken: Faith-Filled Responses to Health Challenges*, we reflect on the insights we've gained about managing fear and anxiety. This week, through the comforting and empowering words of Scripture, we've explored strategies to replace fear and anxiety with peace and trust in God's promises. Each day, we delved into different facets of fear and anxiety, learning how to confront these emotions head-on with the guidance of God's Word.

Practical Tools for Battling Fear and Anxiety

Maintain a Spirit of Joy:

Tool: Practice gratitude. Start or end each day by listing things you are grateful for. This can shift your focus from fear to appreciation, enhancing overall well-being.

Structured Prayer and Meditation:

Tool: Regular prayer sessions. Incorporate specific times for prayer and meditation into your daily routine, focusing on God's promises of protection and provision to combat anxiety.

Cultivate Mindfulness:

Tool: Mindful breathing exercises. Use deep breathing techniques to center your thoughts in the present moment when feeling overwhelmed, reducing anxiety.

Positive Focus:

Tool: Visual reminders. Keep visible reminders around your home or workspace of encouraging Scriptures and uplifting quotes that remind you of God's care and your past victories over anxiety.

Community Support:

Tool: Engage in supportive relationships. Regularly connect with friends, family, or support groups who can provide encouragement and perspective when you're struggling with fear.

Education on Fear and Anxiety

Tool: Read and educate yourself about the physiological and psychological aspects of fear and anxiety. Understanding these can demystify the feelings and make them easier to manage.

Professional Help

Tool: Therapy or counseling. Consider professional help if anxiety becomes overwhelming, providing a structured approach to understanding and managing your fears.

Reflection

Throughout this week, we have learned that fear and anxiety, while natural responses to the uncertainties of health challenges, can be managed effectively through faith and practical action. Each scriptural passage provided us tools and perspectives to help reshape our response to these emotions, guiding us towards a life marked by God's peace rather than our fears.

Prayer for the Week

Dear Lord, thank You for guiding us through another week of learning to trust You more deeply. Please help us to apply the tools we've learned to manage our fears and anxieties. Strengthen us to rely on Your promises and the peace You offer, which surpasses all understanding. Let us remember that we are not alone in our struggles and that You are always with us, offering strength and comfort. In Jesus' name, Amen.

As we move into next week, let's carry with us the lessons of trust and peace, knowing that through God, we can face each day with renewed courage and hope.

WEEK THREE

Rest For Ourselves & Concern for Our Loved Ones

This week is intentionally written not only for those walking through a health challenge, but especially for those who are caring for them. If you are reading these pages as a caregiver, I wish I could give you a giant hug right now. The act of care-giving is often unseen and unrecognized work, but it is essential to your loved one's wellbeing and healing. Lean into the scriptures this week and remember that rest for you is just as important as rest for your loved one battling a health challenge.

Have you ever been so tired that even your sleep felt exhausting? Like you could sleep for a week and still not feel rested? In the relentless pace of managing health challenges, either our own or those of someone we love, finding true rest can seem like a mythical quest—reserved for those untouched by real troubles.

It's easy to isolate, to pull back into our shells like a tortoise and hope the world just passes us by until we can catch our breath. Trust me, I understand this temptation. I give in to it often. But this kind of fatigue, the soul-deep weariness, needs more than sleep; it needs restoration.

Rest is not merely a physical necessity but a divine command that rejuvenates our spirit and enables our bodies to heal as we care for those we love.

In our society, there's a badge of honor associated with busyness. You know what I mean. Being busy often gets equated with being important, being indispensable, or being productive. But here's what living with chronic illness has taught me: you cannot pour from an empty cup. You've probably heard that a thousand times, but let's really think about what this means.

Rest as a Divine Command

In Genesis 2:2-3, after creating the heavens and the earth, God rested on the seventh day. He didn't rest because of fatigue. He rested as an example to us—an eternal principle woven into the fabric of creation. Rest is not about laziness; it's about setting a rhythm to our lives that balances work with restorative pauses.

Then, in Mark 6:31, Jesus says to His disciples, "Come with me by yourselves to a quiet place and get some rest." Notice He didn't just suggest it as a nice idea; He led them to it. It was a moment away from the crowds, away from the miracles, and the constant demand of their ministries. It was a deliberate pause.

Rest to Strengthen Spirit

Rest is powerful. It's not just about catching up on sleep. It's about allowing our minds, bodies, and spirits to renew. Think about Elijah in 1 Kings 19. After a significant spiritual showdown, he fled Jezebel's threats and went into the wilderness. There, under a broom bush, he fell into despair. What did God do? He sent an angel, not to scold him for his fear, but to provide food and water and to let him sleep. Sometimes, the most spiritual thing you can do is rest.

But how do we balance this need for rest with our responsibilities to care for others, especially when we or our loved ones are walking through a health challenge?

The Balancing Act

The world doesn't stop when we encounter a health crisis. Family meals still need to be made. Laundry still needs to washed, dried, folded, and— the hardest part, put away! Children still need to be taken to and picked up from school. Birthdays still need to be celebrated. Toilets still need to be cleaned. Bills still need to be paid. Work still needs to be done. A unique tension arises when battling a health challenge while also maintaining the everyday obligations of life.

My family has walked through this tension several times. During some of our health crisis situations, I didn't have an option in balancing the tension— I was in a coma, in an extended stay at the hospital, or confined to bed rest for recovery. In other situations, I was forced to adjust my schedule and obligations to accommodate more time for rest, healing, or caution in my physical activity.

Caring for others requires energy—emotional, physical, and spiritual energy. But if we're running on empty, how effective can we really be? We've all heard it on airplanes: put on your own oxygen mask before helping others. Why? Because you can't help anyone if you're unconscious. Similarly, we need spiritual and emotional oxygen to care for ourselves and others.

Practical Steps to Rest

1. Schedule It: Just like any important appointment, schedule your rest. It might be an hour where you switch off all devices and read the Bible, pray, or just sit quietly. It might be an afternoon where you do something that rejuvenates you. Protect this time like you would any other important appointment.

2. Set Boundaries: It's okay to say no or not now. That's not selfish; it's wise. Boundaries allow you to regenerate your own strength so you can be fully present for those who need you.

3. Rest in God: Your ultimate rest comes from God. Matthew 11:28 invites us to come to Jesus when we are weary and burdened, and He will give us rest. This is the deep, soul-level rest we crave.

Rest as Worship

Rest also acts as an act of trust and worship. It's saying to God, "I trust that You will hold all things together while I rest." It's recognizing that the world does not rest on our shoulders but His. It acknowledges our human limitations and His infinite power.

As we focus this week on finding the right balance between self-care and caring for others, remember that neglecting your rest doesn't glorify God or serve others effectively. It just leads to burnout.

So, I invite you to join me in learning to rest, really rest. Not just sleep, but to find restoration in God, to set boundaries that protect your peace, and to use your periods of rest to enhance your ability to care for others.

We are on this journey together, learning to balance the weight of our responsibilities with the lightness of His grace. And remember, in Christ, even our rest can be a form of worship, a surrender that says, "God, I trust You with this time with my loved ones, and with my own needs."

This week, let's challenge ourselves to find true rest—not just for our bodies, but for our souls—and see how this strengthens us to be the caretakers and lovers of souls that God has called us to be.

Week 3, Day 1: Find rest for your soul

As we enter Week 3 of *Unshaken: Faith-Filled Responses to Health Challenges*, our focus shifts towards balancing self-care with caring for others, starting with the fundamental concept of rest. Today, we explore Genesis 2:1-3 and Matthew 11:25-30, scriptures that highlight the divine endorsement and personal invitation to rest. In Genesis, God models rest after His work of creation, setting a precedent for its importance. In Matthew, Jesus extends a heartfelt invitation to find rest in Him, specifically targeting those burdened and weary. These passages together remind us that rest is not only a physical necessity but also a spiritual command and comfort.

Genesis 2:1-3

The heavens, the earth, and all their vast array were finished. 2 On the seventh day God finished his work which he had done; and he rested on the seventh day from all his work which he had done. 3 God blessed the seventh day, and made it holy, because he rested in it from all his work of creation which he had done.

Matthew 11:25-30

At that time, Jesus answered, "I thank you, Father, Lord of heaven and earth, that you hid these things from the wise and understanding, and revealed them to infants. 26 Yes, Father, for so it was well-pleasing in your sight. 27 All things have been delivered to me by my Father. No one knows the Son, except the Father; neither does anyone know the Father, except the Son and he to whom the Son desires to reveal him.

28 "Come to me, all you who labor and are heavily burdened, and I will give you rest. 29 Take my yoke upon you and learn from me, for I am gentle and humble in heart; and you will find rest for your souls. 30 For my yoke is easy, and my burden is light."

Journaling Questions

Spend a few moments today reflecting on the Scripture above, writing down any insights, questions, or prayers that come to mind.

1. Genesis 2:1-3 tells us that even God rested on the seventh day after His work of creation. How does this divine example of rest influence your views on the need for rest in your own life, especially when dealing with health challenges?

2. In Matthew 11:28, Jesus invites us to come to Him to find rest. Reflect on a time when you turned to spiritual practices (like prayer or reading scripture) for rest and rejuvenation. How did this spiritual rest impact your physical and emotional state?

3. Consider the yoke that Jesus talks about in Matthew 11:29-30. How can exchanging your burdens for Christ's yoke help you find rest in the midst of health challenges? What does taking His yoke upon you imply in your daily life?

4. Discuss the balance between resting and remaining active in managing your health. How can you implement rest as a regular part of your health regimen without feeling guilty or neglectful of your responsibilities?

5. Reflect on the statement, "For my yoke is easy and my burden is light." How can embracing this truth change your approach to rest, particularly in times of stress or illness? How might this perspective alleviate feelings of overwhelm or fatigue in caring for yourself and others?

Week 3, Day 2: A Sabbath rest for the people of God

On our second day of focusing on rest and care, we turn to Hebrews 4:1-13, which underscores the spiritual significance of rest as an act of worship and obedience. This passage speaks of a "Sabbath rest" for the people of God, emphasizing that entering God's rest means trusting in His work rather than our own. The text invites us to lay aside our efforts and to trust in the finished work of Christ, illustrating how true rest—both physical and spiritual—is foundational to our faith. As we navigate our health challenges, understanding rest as an integral part of worship helps us align our lives with God's rhythms of grace and renewal.

Hebrews 4:1-13

Let's fear therefore, lest perhaps anyone of you should seem to have come short of a promise of entering into his rest. 2 For indeed we have had good news preached to us, even as they also did, but the word they heard didn't profit them, because it wasn't mixed with faith by those who heard. 3 For we who have believed do enter into that rest, even as he has said, "As I swore in my wrath, they will not enter into my rest;" although the works were finished from the foundation of the world. 4 For he has said this somewhere about the seventh day, "God rested on the seventh day from all his works;" 5 and in this place again, "They will not enter into my rest."

6 Seeing therefore it remains that some should enter into it, and they to whom the good news was preached before failed to enter in because of disobedience, 7 he again defines a certain day, "today", saying through David so long a time afterward (just as has been said),
"Today if you will hear his voice,
don't harden your hearts."

8 For if Joshua had given them rest, he would not have spoken afterward of another day. 9 There remains therefore a Sabbath rest for the people of God. 10 For he who has entered into his rest has himself also rested from his works, as God did from his. 11 Let's therefore give diligence to enter into that rest, lest anyone fall after the same example of disobedience. 12 For the word of God is living and active, and sharper than any two-edged sword, piercing even to the dividing of soul and spirit, of both joints and marrow, and is able to discern the thoughts and intentions of the heart. 13 There is no creature that is hidden from his sight, but all things are naked and laid open before the eyes of him to whom we must give an account.

Journaling Questions

Spend a few moments today reflecting on the Scripture above, writing down any insights, questions, or prayers that come to mind.

1. Hebrews 4:1-2 discusses the promise of entering God's rest and the need for faith to access it. How can viewing rest as a faithful response to God's promise change your approach to taking time out for rest amid health challenges?

2. "For anyone who enters God's rest also rests from their works, just as God did from his" (v.10). Reflect on how you can implement this principle in your life, especially when you feel compelled to keep busy despite health concerns. What might "resting from your works" look like for you?

3. The passage warns about the danger of disobedience and the example of Israel who did not enter God's rest because of unbelief (v.11). How does this relate to your own experiences of rest or the lack thereof? Are there areas where unbelief or disobedience makes it difficult for you to rest?

4. Verses 12-13 describe God's word as living and active, discerning our innermost thoughts and desires. How can this understanding of God's knowledge of your needs encourage you to prioritize rest? How might it help you to deal with any guilt associated with resting?

5. Consider the broader implications of rest in your relationships and service to others. How can ensuring you are well-rested impact your ability to care for and support others? How does it enhance your worship and service to God?

_____

_____

_____

_____

_____

_____

_____

_____

_____

_____

_____

_____

_____

_____

_____

_____

Week 3, Day 3: Walk in love

As we continue our exploration of rest and care, today's focus shifts to how we can support loved ones facing health challenges. Colossians 3:12-17 provides profound guidance on embodying compassion, kindness, humility, gentleness, and patience—qualities essential for nurturing relationships during difficult times. This passage not only calls us to bear with each other and forgive one another but also to let the peace of Christ rule in our hearts and be thankful. As we reflect on these verses, let's consider how these instructions can strengthen our ability to care for others who are struggling, reminding us that our interactions can be powerful expressions of love and support.

Colossians 3:12-17

12 Put on therefore, as God's chosen ones, holy and beloved, a heart of compassion, kindness, lowliness, humility, and perseverance; 13 bearing with one another, and forgiving each other, if any man has a complaint against any; even as Christ forgave you, so you also do.

14 Above all these things, walk in love, which is the bond of perfection. 15 And let the peace of God rule in your hearts, to which also you were called in one body, and be thankful. 16 Let the word of Christ dwell in you richly; in all wisdom teaching and admonishing one another with psalms, hymns, and spiritual songs, singing with grace in your heart to the Lord.

17 Whatever you do, in word or in deed, do all in the name of the Lord Jesus, giving thanks to God the Father through him.

Journaling Questions

Spend a few moments today reflecting on the Scripture above, writing down any insights, questions, or prayers that come to mind.

1. "Therefore, as God's chosen people, holy and dearly loved, clothe yourselves with compassion, kindness, humility, gentleness and patience" (v.12). How can you apply these virtues in your daily interactions with a loved one who is facing health challenges? Can you share a recent instance where embodying one of these traits made a difference?

2. Reflect on the command to bear with each other and forgive one another (v.13). How does this approach help in managing the stress and strain that can come from the health challenges of loved ones? What are some practical ways you can cultivate forgiveness and understanding in these situations?

3. "And over all these virtues put on love, which binds them all together in perfect unity" (v.14). Discuss how love plays a role in supporting others through their health challenges. How does love influence your actions and decisions when caring for someone?

4. The peace of Christ is meant to rule in our hearts (v.15). How can maintaining peace within yourself impact your ability to support others? What strategies can you use to ensure that you remain a calming and stabilizing presence for those in need?

5. "Let the message of Christ dwell among you richly" (v.16). How can sharing your faith and the truths of Scripture provide comfort and encouragement to those experiencing health challenges? Consider ways you might integrate spiritual encouragement into your support efforts.

_____

_____

_____

_____

_____

_____

_____

_____

_____

_____

_____

_____

_____

_____

_____

_____

_____

_____

Week 3, Day 4: The width and length and height and depth

      Today we delve into the depths of Ephesians 3:14-21, where Paul prays for the Ephesians to comprehend the vastness of Christ's love—a love that surpasses knowledge. This passage is a powerful reminder that God's love for our loved ones is not only greater than our own but is immeasurable and perfect. As we consider the challenges our loved ones face, whether health-related or otherwise, understanding the scope of God's love can bring immense comfort and trust. It reassures us that they are cared for far beyond our capabilities. Let's reflect on this boundless love and how it can affect our perspectives and responses when supporting those we care about.

Ephesians 3:14-21

14 For this cause, I bow my knees to the Father of our Lord Jesus Christ, 15 from whom every family in heaven and on earth is named, 16 that he would grant you, according to the riches of his glory, that you may be strengthened with power through his Spirit in the inner person, 17 that Christ may dwell in your hearts through faith, to the end that you, being rooted and grounded in love, 18 may be strengthened to comprehend with all the saints what is the width and length and height and depth, 19 and to know Christ's love which surpasses knowledge, that you may be filled with all the fullness of God.

20 Now to him who is able to do exceedingly abundantly above all that we ask or think, according to the power that works in us, 21 to him be the glory in the assembly and in Christ Jesus to all generations, forever and ever. Amen.

Journaling Questions

      Spend a few moments today reflecting on the Scripture above, writing down any insights, questions, or prayers that come to mind.

1. "I pray that you, being rooted and established in love, may have power, together with all the Lord's holy people, to grasp how wide and long and high and deep is the love of Christ" (v.17-18). How does understanding the magnitude of Christ's love for your loved ones change your own feelings of worry or anxiety about their well-being?

2. Reflect on the phrase "to know this love that surpasses knowledge" (v.19). How can embracing the idea that God's love surpasses our own understanding provide peace when you think about the care and future of your loved ones?

3. Consider how Paul's desire for the Ephesians to be "filled to the measure of all the fullness of God" (v.19) can be a prayer for those you care about. How might this prayer influence the way you support and interact with loved ones facing health challenges?

4. Paul speaks about God's ability to do "immeasurably more than all we ask or imagine" (v.20). How can keeping this promise in mind encourage you when you feel limited in how much you can help a loved one?

5. Discuss ways you can foster a deeper trust in God's care for your loved ones, especially in times when their health challenges seem overwhelming. How can this trust impact your actions and emotional responses?

_____

_____

_____

_____

_____

_____

_____

_____

_____

_____

_____

_____

_____

_____

_____

_____

_____

_____

Week 3, Day 5: Comfort, comfort my people

On the final day of this week's focus, we turn to Isaiah 40, a chapter rich with promises of God's enduring strength and renewal for those who wait on Him. This scripture famously assures us that even youths grow tired and weary, but those who hope in the Lord will renew their strength; they will soar on wings like eagles, run and not grow weary, walk and not be faint. As we consider our roles in supporting loved ones through health challenges, let's reflect on how prioritizing rest is not only a form of self-care but also a crucial strategy for maintaining our ability to care for others effectively.

Isaiah 40

1 "Comfort, comfort my people," says your God.
2 "Speak comfortably to Jerusalem, and call out to her that her warfare is accomplished, that her iniquity is pardoned,
that she has received of the LORD's hand double for all her sins."
3 The voice of one who calls out,
"Prepare the way of the LORD in the wilderness!
Make a level highway in the desert for our God.
4 Every valley shall be exalted,
and every mountain and hill shall be made low.
The uneven shall be made level,
and the rough places a plain.
5 The LORD's glory shall be revealed,
and all flesh shall see it together;
for the mouth of the LORD has spoken it."

6 The voice of one saying, "Cry out!"
One said, "What shall I cry?"
"All flesh is like grass,
and all its glory is like the flower of the field.
7 The grass withers,
the flower fades,
because the LORD's breath blows on it.
Surely the people are like grass.
8 The grass withers,
the flower fades;
but the word of our God stands forever."

9 You who tell good news to Zion, go up on a high mountain.
You who tell good news to Jerusalem, lift up your voice with strength!
Lift it up! Don't be afraid!
Say to the cities of Judah, "Behold, your God!"
10 Behold, the Lord GOD will come as a mighty one,
and his arm will rule for him.
Behold, his reward is with him,
and his recompense before him.
11 He will feed his flock like a shepherd.
He will gather the lambs in his arm,
and carry them in his bosom.
He will gently lead those who have their young.

12 Who has measured the waters in the hollow of his hand,
and marked off the sky with his span,
and calculated the dust of the earth in a measuring basket,
and weighed the mountains in scales,
and the hills in a balance?
13 Who has directed the LORD's Spirit,
or has taught him as his counselor?
14 Who did he take counsel with,
and who instructed him,
and taught him in the path of justice,
and taught him knowledge,
and showed him the way of understanding?
15 Behold, the nations are like a drop in a bucket,
and are regarded as a speck of dust on a balance.
Behold, he lifts up the islands like a very little thing.
16 Lebanon is not sufficient to burn,
nor its animals sufficient for a burnt offering.
17 All the nations are like nothing before him.
They are regarded by him as less than nothing, and vanity.

18 To whom then will you liken God?
Or what likeness will you compare to him?
19 A workman has cast an image,
and the goldsmith overlays it with gold,
and casts silver chains for it.
20 He who is too impoverished for such an offering chooses a tree that will not rot.
He seeks a skillful workman to set up a carved image for him that will not be moved.

21 Haven't you known?
Haven't you heard?
Haven't you been told from the beginning?
Haven't you understood from the foundations of the earth?
22 It is he who sits above the circle of the earth,
and its inhabitants are like grasshoppers;
who stretches out the heavens like a curtain,
and spreads them out like a tent to dwell in,
23 who brings princes to nothing,
who makes the judges of the earth meaningless.
24 They are planted scarcely.
They are sown scarcely.
Their stock has scarcely taken root in the ground.
He merely blows on them, and they wither,
and the whirlwind takes them away as stubble.

25 "To whom then will you liken me?
Who is my equal?" says the Holy One.
26 Lift up your eyes on high,
and see who has created these,
who brings out their army by number.
He calls them all by name.
By the greatness of his might,
and because he is strong in power,
not one is lacking.

27 Why do you say, Jacob,
and speak, Israel,
"My way is hidden from the LORD,
and the justice due me is disregarded by my God"?
28 Haven't you known?
Haven't you heard?
The everlasting God, the LORD,
the Creator of the ends of the earth, doesn't faint.
He isn't weary.
His understanding is unsearchable.

29 He gives power to the weak.
He increases the strength of him who has no might.
30 Even the youths faint and get weary,
and the young men utterly fall;
31 but those who wait for the LORD will renew their strength.
They will mount up with wings like eagles.
They will run, and not be weary.
They will walk, and not faint.

Journaling Questions

Spend a few moments today reflecting on the Scripture above, writing down any insights, questions, or prayers that come to mind.

1. How does the promise that God does not grow tired or weary (Isaiah 40:28) influence your understanding of divine support in your caregiving duties? How can you draw on this divine energy in practical ways?

2. "He gives strength to the weary and increases the power of the weak" (Isaiah 40:29). Reflect on a time when you felt physically or emotionally drained from caring for someone. How can integrating more rest into your routine enable you to find renewal and continue providing support?

3. "Those who hope in the Lord will renew their strength" (Isaiah 40:31). How does placing your hope in God, rather than solely in your own efforts, help you find rest? Discuss how this spiritual rest can impact your capacity to care for others.

4. Consider the imagery of soaring on wings like eagles (Isaiah 40:31). How can this metaphor inspire you to find balance between activity and rest in your life, especially in stressful times?

5. Reflect on the relationship between physical rest and spiritual renewal described in Isaiah 40. How can ensuring adequate rest for yourself help you manifest more patience, compassion, and love towards those you support? What changes might you need to make to better prioritize this rest?

_____

_____

_____

_____

_____

Week 3 Wrap-Up

As we close Week 3 of *Unshaken: Faith-Filled Responses to Health Challenges*, we reflect on the intertwined themes of self-care through rest and the care for others facing health challenges. This week, we've explored how rest is not only beneficial but essential—it rejuvenates our spirit and strengthens our ability to provide support. Let's summarize the practical tools and strategies we've discussed to help us integrate these insights into our lives more effectively.

Practical Tools for Prioritizing Rest and Caring for Loved Ones

Scheduled Rest:

Tool: Calendar Blocks. Dedicate specific times in your weekly schedule strictly for rest, marked clearly in your calendar as non-negotiable appointments with yourself.

Spiritual Renewal:

Tool: Daily Devotionals. Set aside time each day for spiritual activities that rejuvenate your soul, such as prayer, meditation, or reading scripture. This spiritual rest can provide the strength needed to care for others.

Physical Rejuvenation:

Tool: Regular Exercise and Healthy Diet. Engage in light to moderate exercise that you enjoy and eat a balanced diet to improve your overall energy levels and well-being.

Emotional Support:

Tool: Support Networks. Establish and maintain a support network of friends, family, or community members who understand your role as a caregiver and can offer emotional and practical support.

Educational Encouragement:

Tool: Informative Resources. Continually educate yourself about your loved one's health condition through books, reputable online sources, or discussions with medical professionals. This knowledge can help you provide better support and feel more in control.

Delegation and Boundaries

Tool: Task Sharing. Identify tasks that can be shared with others to lighten your load, and be clear about your limits to prevent burnout.

Reflection

Throughout this week, the scriptures and discussions have reminded us that caring for ourselves and others must be a balanced endeavor. By prioritizing rest and using these practical tools, we can ensure that we are not only giving the best of ourselves to our loved ones but also maintaining our own health and well-being.

Prayer for the Week

Heavenly Father, thank You for the lessons of this week on the importance of rest and the care of our loved ones. Help us to apply the tools we've learned to effectively manage our responsibilities and to find rejuvenation in You. Grant us the wisdom to recognize when we need to rest and the strength to support those we love in their times of need. We ask for Your guidance to continue nurturing ourselves and others with compassion and love. In Jesus' name, Amen.

As we move forward, let's carry these tools and insights with us, ensuring that we are equipped to face the challenges of caregiving with a renewed spirit and a healthy balance.

WEEK FOUR

The Bigger Picture - This Was Never Just About You

As we enter the final week of our journey through *Unshaken: Faith-Filled Responses to Health Challenges*, we confront a profound truth: our individual stories of struggle and triumph are not isolated chapters. Instead, they are integral parts of a much larger, divine narrative that God is writing not only in our lives but through our lives. This week, we explore how our personal health challenges connect to a broader purpose and how our experiences can have ripple effects beyond our immediate understanding.

Your story is part of God's grand story. It's easy to feel that our health battles are just about us, our pain, our discomfort, our survival. But what if there's more? What if every tear we shed waters a seed of future hope for someone else? What if our endurance through pain is a lesson in courage for onlookers we may never meet?

The Divine Narrative

In Romans 8:28, we are reminded that "all things work together for good for those who love God, who are called according to his purpose." This scripture isn't minimizing our pain or suggesting that the suffering itself is good; rather, it's pointing to the interconnectedness of our experiences within God's sovereign plan. Our trials are not meaningless; they are purposeful and potent, contributing to a greater good we might only glimpse in eternity.

Learning Through Suffering

Consider Joseph's story in Genesis. His journey from the pit to the palace was fraught with injustice, betrayal, and loneliness. Yet, every painful event was a brushstroke in a masterpiece that would save nations and restore a family. Joseph later said to his brothers, "You intended to harm me, but God intended it for good to accomplish what is now being done, the saving of many lives" (Genesis 50:20). Our struggles too, however deeply personal, have the potential to contribute to God's grander purposes—perhaps even the saving of many lives.

Practical Reflections

1. Record Your Journey: Keep a journal of your experiences, not just as a personal outlet, but as a future resource for others. Documenting your trials, triumphs, and spiritual insights can become a roadmap for those who walk a similar path.

2. Share Your Story: Whether through writing, sharing your testimony or simply conversational sharing, let others know how you've seen God work in your life. Your testimony of His faithfulness through a health challenge can be a powerful tool in God's hands.

3. Stay Open to Purpose: Ask God to show you how your experience can serve a larger purpose. Remain open to opportunities to serve, encourage, or educate others because of what you've endured.

Rest in the Assurance

As we reflect on our journey, we rest in the assurance that our lives are woven into the tapestry of God's eternal purpose. In 2 Corinthians 4:17, Paul calls our afflictions "light and momentary troubles" that are achieving for us an eternal glory that far outweighs them all. This perspective doesn't trivialize our pain but invites us to view it through the lens of eternity.

In God's story, every line matters, every character is crucial, and every plot twist is planned. Your health challenges, your battles, your victories—they matter not just for you but for the countless others who will find courage in your courage, strength in your strength, and hope in your hope.

This week, let's embrace our place in God's narrative, trusting that the same God who writes our stories uses them to paint a picture far grander than we could ever imagine.

Week 4, Day 1: Our hope is steadfast

As we begin the final week of our study, our focus shifts to understanding how our personal trials are part of a much larger, divine narrative. Today, we delve into 2 Corinthians 1:3-11, where Paul discusses the concept of comfort in affliction. In this passage, Paul explains that the comfort we receive from God during our trials is not meant solely for us; rather, it equips us to offer comfort to others facing similar situations. This perspective helps us see our health challenges not just as personal trials but as opportunities to serve and uplift others, integrating our experiences into God's broader purpose.

2 Corinthians 1:3-11

Blessed be the God and Father of our Lord Jesus Christ, the Father of mercies and God of all comfort, 4 who comforts us in all our affliction, that we may be able to comfort those who are in any affliction, through the comfort with which we ourselves are comforted by God. 5 For as the sufferings of Christ abound to us, even so our comfort also abounds through Christ. 6 But if we are afflicted, it is for your comfort and salvation. If we are comforted, it is for your comfort, which produces in you the patient enduring of the same sufferings which we also suffer. 7 Our hope for you is steadfast, knowing that, since you are partakers of the sufferings, so you are also of the comfort.

8 For we don't desire to have you uninformed, brothers, concerning our affliction which happened to us in Asia: that we were weighed down exceedingly, beyond our power, so much that we despaired even of life. 9 Yes, we ourselves have had the sentence of death within ourselves, that we should not trust in ourselves, but in God who raises the dead, 10 who delivered us out of so great a death, and does deliver, on whom we have set our hope that he will also still deliver us, 11 you also helping together on our behalf by your supplication; that, for the gift given to us by means of many, thanks may be given by many persons on your behalf.

Journaling Questions

Spend a few moments today reflecting on the Scripture above, writing down any insights, questions, or prayers that come to mind.

1. "The Father of compassion and the God of all comfort, who comforts us in all our troubles" (v.3-4). Reflect on a time when you experienced God's comfort in the midst of a health challenge. How can you use that experience to comfort someone else who might be facing similar difficulties?

2. Paul shares that the comfort received is meant to be shared with others in any affliction (v.4). How does knowing that your trials could help others influence your perspective on your own health challenges?

3. "If we are distressed, it is for your comfort and salvation" (v.6). Consider how your personal struggles with health could potentially be beneficial to others. Can you think of any specific instances where your experience has already helped or could help someone else?

4. In verses 8-9, Paul speaks about being burdened excessively, beyond his ability, so that he would learn to rely not on himself but on God. How has relying on God through your health challenges prepared you to support others? How does this reliance manifest in your ability to comfort others?

5. Paul discusses the hope they have for their deliverance (v.10). How can maintaining hope in the face of ongoing health issues empower you to become a source of hope for others? What steps can you take to cultivate and share this hope more actively?

_____

_____

_____

_____

_____

_____

_____

_____

_____

_____

_____

_____

_____

_____

_____

_____

_____

_____

Week 4, Day 2: I glory in my weakness

Today, we examine 2 Corinthians 12:1-10, where Paul discusses his own vulnerabilities and how they serve as a stage for showcasing God's strength. In this poignant passage, Paul describes a "thorn in his flesh" that he pleaded with the Lord to take away. God's response, "My grace is sufficient for you, for my power is made perfect in weakness," provides a transformative perspective on suffering and limitations. As we consider our health challenges, this scripture encourages us to see our weaknesses not as mere hindrances but as opportunities for God's power to be vividly displayed in our lives.

2 Corinthians 12:1-10

1 It is doubtless not profitable for me to boast, but I will come to visions and revelations of the Lord. 2 I know a man in Christ who was caught up into the third heaven fourteen years ago—whether in the body, I don't know, or whether out of the body, I don't know; God knows. 3 I know such a man (whether in the body, or outside of the body, I don't know; God knows), 4 how he was caught up into Paradise and heard unspeakable words, which it is not lawful for a man to utter. 5 On behalf of such a one I will boast, but on my own behalf I will not boast, except in my weaknesses. 6 For if I would desire to boast, I will not be foolish; for I will speak the truth. But I refrain, so that no man may think more of me than that which he sees in me or hears from me. 7 By reason of the exceeding greatness of the revelations, that I should not be exalted excessively, a thorn in the flesh was given to me: a messenger of Satan to torment me, that I should not be exalted excessively. 8 Concerning this thing, I begged the Lord three times that it might depart from me. 9 He has said to me, "My grace is sufficient for you, for my power is made perfect in weakness." Most gladly therefore I will rather glory in my weaknesses, that the power of Christ may rest on me.

10 Therefore I take pleasure in weaknesses, in injuries, in necessities, in persecutions, and in distresses, for Christ's sake. For when I am weak, then am I strong.

Journaling Questions

Spend a few moments today reflecting on the Scripture above, writing down any insights, questions, or prayers that come to mind.

1. "My grace is sufficient for you, for my power is made perfect in weakness" (v.9). Reflect on how this statement might change your view of your own weaknesses or health challenges. How can you embrace your limitations as opportunities for God's strength to shine through?

2. Paul takes pleasure in his weaknesses because Christ's power rests on him (v.9-10). How can adopting a similar attitude affect your approach to health challenges? Can you think of instances where embracing your weaknesses could lead to greater spiritual or personal growth?

3. Consider how the concept of power in weakness can be communicated to others who are struggling. How might your experiences provide comfort or inspiration to someone feeling overwhelmed by their own health issues?

4. Discuss the interplay between asking for healing and accepting God's sufficient grace. How do you balance prayer for relief with acceptance of God's plan for your strengths and weaknesses?

5. "Therefore I will boast all the more gladly about my weaknesses" (v.9). How can openly sharing your struggles and vulnerabilities act as a testimony to others about the strength and sufficiency of God's grace? How does this openness impact your relationships and ability to minister to others?

Week 4, Day 3: Count it all joy

In today's focus, we explore James 1:1-18, where James discusses the transformative power of enduring trials and the wisdom that comes from these experiences. James encourages believers to consider it pure joy when they face various trials because the testing of faith develops perseverance, which must finish its work so that they may be mature and complete, lacking nothing. This perspective frames our health challenges as not merely obstacles but as opportunities to gain profound wisdom and spiritual maturity. As we navigate our own difficulties, let's consider how these trials are shaping us into wiser, more resilient individuals.

James 1:1-18

1 James, a servant of God and of the Lord Jesus Christ, to the twelve tribes which are in the Dispersion: Greetings.

2 Count it all joy, my brothers, when you fall into various temptations, 3 knowing that the testing of your faith produces endurance. 4 Let endurance have its perfect work, that you may be perfect and complete, lacking in nothing.

5 But if any of you lacks wisdom, let him ask of God, who gives to all liberally and without reproach, and it will be given to him. 6 But let him ask in faith, without any doubting, for he who doubts is like a wave of the sea, driven by the wind and tossed. 7 For that man shouldn't think that he will receive anything from the Lord. 8 He is a double-minded man, unstable in all his ways.

9 Let the brother in humble circumstances glory in his high position; 10 and the rich, in that he is made humble, because like the flower in the grass, he will pass away. 11 For the sun arises with the scorching wind and withers the grass; and the flower in it falls, and the beauty of its appearance perishes. So the rich man will also fade away in his pursuits. 12 Blessed is a person who endures temptation, for when he has been approved, he will receive the crown of life which the Lord promised to those who love him.

13 Let no man say when he is tempted, "I am tempted by God," for God can't be tempted by evil, and he himself tempts no one. 14 But each one is tempted when he is drawn away by his own lust and enticed. 15 Then the lust, when it has conceived, bears sin. The sin, when it is full grown, produces death. 16 Don't be deceived, my beloved brothers. 17 Every good gift and every perfect gift is from above, coming down from the Father of lights, with whom can be no variation nor turning shadow. 18 Of his own will he gave birth to us by the word of truth, that we should be a kind of first fruits of his creatures.

Journaling Questions

Spend a few moments today reflecting on the Scripture above, writing down any insights, questions, or prayers that come to mind.

1. "Consider it pure joy, my brothers and sisters, whenever you face trials of many kinds" (v.2). How can you apply this instruction to your health challenges? What shifts in perspective are needed to view these difficulties as opportunities for joy?

2. "The testing of your faith produces perseverance" (v.3). Reflect on a specific health challenge you've faced. How has this experience tested your faith and what lessons in perseverance have you learned?

3. James advises seeking wisdom from God, who gives generously to all without finding fault (v.5). How can you actively seek wisdom in your situation? What specific prayers or actions might help you gain the wisdom you need to navigate your health challenges more effectively?

4. "Blessed is the one who perseveres under trial because, having stood the test, that person will receive the crown of life that the Lord has promised to those who love him" (v.12). How does this promise affect your endurance? How might this assurance change your approach to ongoing health issues?

5. Consider the role of wisdom in managing your responses to health challenges. How has your understanding of wisdom changed through your experiences? What practical steps can you take to further cultivate wisdom in your life?

Week 4, Day 4: Light will shine out of darkness

As we near the end of our study, today's scripture, 2 Corinthians 4:1-18, encourages us to shift our focus from the temporal to the eternal. In this passage, Paul speaks about the challenges and persecutions he faces, yet he emphasizes the importance of not losing heart. Despite the outer decay, he highlights the renewal happening within us day by day and the eternal glory that far outweighs any present troubles when we fix our eyes not on what is seen, but on what is unseen. This perspective is crucial as we deal with health challenges, reminding us to look beyond our current struggles to the eternal hope and promise in Christ.

2 Corinthians 4:1-18

1 Therefore, seeing we have this ministry, even as we obtained mercy, we don't faint. 2 But we have renounced the hidden things of shame, not walking in craftiness nor handling the word of God deceitfully, but by the manifestation of the truth commending ourselves to every man's conscience in the sight of God. 3 Even if our Good News is veiled, it is veiled in those who are dying, 4 in whom the god of this world has blinded the minds of the unbelieving, that the light of the Good News of the glory of Christ, who is the image of God, should not dawn on them. 5 For we don't preach ourselves, but Christ Jesus as Lord, and ourselves as your servants for Jesus' sake, 6 seeing it is God who said, "Light will shine out of darkness," who has shone in our hearts to give the light of the knowledge of the glory of God in the face of Jesus Christ.

7 But we have this treasure in clay vessels, that the exceeding greatness of the power may be of God and not from ourselves. 8 We are pressed on every side, yet not crushed; perplexed, yet not to despair; 9 pursued, yet not forsaken; struck down, yet not destroyed; 10 always carrying in the body the putting to death of the Lord Jesus, that the life of Jesus may also be revealed in our body. 11 For we who live are always delivered to death for Jesus' sake, that the life also of Jesus may be revealed in our mortal flesh. 12 So then death works in us, but life in you.

13 But having the same spirit of faith, according to that which is written, "I believed, and therefore I spoke." We also believe, and therefore we also speak, 14 knowing that he who raised the Lord Jesus will raise us also with Jesus, and will present us with you. 15 For all things are for your sakes, that the grace, being multiplied through the many, may cause the thanksgiving to abound to the glory of God.

16 Therefore we don't faint, but though our outward person is decaying, yet our inward person is renewed day by day. 17 For our light affliction, which is for the moment, works for us more and more exceedingly an eternal weight of glory, 18 while we don't look at the things which are seen, but at the things which are not seen. For the things which are seen are temporal, but the things which are not seen are eternal.

Journaling Questions

Spend a few moments today reflecting on the Scripture above, writing down any insights, questions, or prayers that come to mind.

1. Consider the statement that the life of Jesus may be revealed in our mortal body (v.11). How can your health challenges and how you handle them serve as a testimony to the life and power of Jesus? What steps can you take to ensure that your life reflects this even in times of difficulty?

2. Reflect on how your understanding of affliction as being for God's glory might transform your approach to suffering (v.15). How does seeing your trials as opportunities to glorify God influence your attitude towards them?

3. "Therefore we do not lose heart. Though outwardly we are wasting away, yet inwardly we are being renewed day by day" (v.16). How does this verse help you to cope with the physical or emotional wear of health challenges? In what ways can you focus more on your inner renewal?

4. Paul contrasts the light and momentary troubles with the eternal glory that far outweighs them all (v.17). How can maintaining an eternal perspective change your daily experience and response to health challenges?

5. "So we fix our eyes not on what is seen, but on what is unseen, since what is seen is temporary, but what is unseen is eternal" (v.18). What are some practical ways you can shift your focus from your current health issues to the eternal promises of God?

Week 4, Day 5: We rejoice in hope of the glory of God

On the final day of our study, we reflect on Romans 5, a passage that encapsulates the essence of hope, peace, and joy through Christ, even amidst suffering. Paul explains that suffering produces perseverance; perseverance, character; and character, hope. This hope does not put us to shame because God's love has been poured out into our hearts through the Holy Spirit. As we navigate health challenges, this scripture invites us to see them as part of a greater divine narrative where suffering has a purpose, and where peace, joy, and eternal life are promised through our faith in Christ.

Romans 5

1 Being therefore justified by faith, we have peace with God through our Lord Jesus Christ; 2 through whom we also have our access by faith into this grace in which we stand. We rejoice in hope of the glory of God. 3 Not only this, but we also rejoice in our sufferings, knowing that suffering produces perseverance; 4 and perseverance, proven character; and proven character, hope; 5 and hope doesn't disappoint us, because God's love has been poured into our hearts through the Holy Spirit who was given to us.

6 For while we were yet weak, at the right time Christ died for the ungodly. 7 For one will hardly die for a righteous man. Yet perhaps for a good person someone would even dare to die. 8 But God commends his own love toward us, in that while we were yet sinners, Christ died for us.

9 Much more then, being now justified by his blood, we will be saved from God's wrath through him. 10 For if while we were enemies, we were reconciled to God through the death of his Son, much more, being reconciled, we will be saved by his life.

11 Not only so, but we also rejoice in God through our Lord Jesus Christ, through whom we have now received the reconciliation. 12 Therefore, as sin entered into the world through one man, and death through sin, so death passed to all men because all sinned. 13 For until the law, sin was in the world; but sin is not charged when there is no law. 14 Nevertheless death reigned from Adam until Moses, even over those whose sins weren't like Adam's disobedience, who is a foreshadowing of him who was to come.

15 But the free gift isn't like the trespass. For if by the trespass of the one the many died, much more did the grace of God and the gift by the grace of the one man, Jesus Christ, abound to the many. 16 The gift is not as through one who sinned; for the judgment came by one to condemnation, but the free gift followed many trespasses to justification. 17 For if by the trespass of the one, death reigned through the one; so much more will those who receive the abundance of grace and of the gift of righteousness reign in life through the one, Jesus Christ.

18 So then as through one trespass, all men were condemned; even so through one act of righteousness, all men were justified to life. 19 For as through the one man's disobedience many were made sinners, even so through the obedience of the one, many will be made righteous. 20 The law came in that the trespass might abound; but where sin abounded, grace abounded more exceedingly, 21 that as sin reigned in death, even so grace might reign through righteousness to eternal life through Jesus Christ our Lord.'

Journaling Questions

Spend a few moments today reflecting on the Scripture above, writing down any insights, questions, or prayers that come to mind.

1. "Since we have been justified through faith, we have peace with God through our Lord Jesus Christ" (v.1). How does understanding that you have peace with God alter your response to health challenges? How can this assurance affect your daily life?

2. Paul discusses rejoicing in our sufferings because suffering produces perseverance (v.3). Reflect on a personal experience where a health challenge led to perseverance. How did this experience strengthen your character and deepen your hope?

3. "Hope does not put us to shame, because God's love has been poured out into our hearts through the Holy Spirit" (v.5). How can remembering that God's love is continually poured into your life inspire you during difficult times? What are some ways you can remind yourself of this truth when facing health challenges?

4. Consider the ultimate sacrifice of Christ discussed in v.6-8. How does the realization that Christ died for us while we were still sinners help you grasp the depth of His love and commitment to your well-being?

5. "We also boast in God through our Lord Jesus Christ, through whom we have now received reconciliation" (v.11). How does the concept of reconciliation with God bring peace and joy to your life, especially in the context of health issues? How can this peace and joy be shared with others who are struggling?

Week 4 Wrap Up

As we conclude our four-week journey through *Unshaken: Faith-Filled Responses to Health Challenges*, this final week has focused on understanding how our individual health challenges fit into a larger, divine narrative. We have explored how these difficulties not only shape us but also prepare us to serve a greater purpose. This week, we've delved into scriptures that help us see our trials from an eternal perspective, emphasizing the transformational aspects of suffering and the ultimate peace, joy, and life we find in Christ. Let's review some practical tools that can help us shift our focus from our immediate struggles to the broader implications and opportunities they present.

Practical Tools for Shifting Our Perspective

Developing a Theology of Suffering

Tool: Study and reflect on biblical teachings about suffering. Understanding the purpose and role of trials in the Christian life can help you view your health challenges through a lens of spiritual growth and opportunity.

Maintaining an Eternal Perspective:

Tool: Regular meditation on Scriptures that highlight eternal promises. Keeping verses like Romans 8:18 ("I consider that our present sufferings are not worth comparing with the glory that will be revealed in us") in mind can help maintain focus on the eternal rather than the temporal.

Journaling for Reflection and Insight:

Tool: Keep a journal to reflect on how your trials are shaping you and potentially preparing you to help others. This can transform your view of suffering from something purely negative to a valuable tool for growth and empathy.

Engagement in Community Support:

Tool: Actively participate in community groups, such as church small groups or support groups for those with similar health issues. Sharing your experiences can shift your perspective from an inward focus to seeing how your journey impacts others.

Service and Volunteering:

Tool: When and if you are ready, engage in volunteer opportunities to help others, even within your capacity limitations. Service can be a powerful way to see the value and purpose in your experiences, particularly how they equip you to empathize and aid others.

Reflection

Throughout this week, and indeed over the entire course of this study, we've been reminded that our struggles, while personal and often painful, are also pathways to deeper faith, greater empathy, and more profound spiritual insights. By embracing these perspectives and employing these tools, we can ensure that our journey through health challenges is not just about endurance, but about enrichment and purpose.

Prayer for the Week

Heavenly Father, thank You for walking with us through this study and through each step of our health challenges. We ask for the strength to continue applying what we've learned, to shift our focus from our immediate pain to the greater purpose You have for us. Help us to embrace our trials as opportunities to display Your power, share Your comfort, and live out the hope we have in Christ. May we be lights in the darkness, bearing witness to Your strength in our weakness. In Jesus' name, Amen.

As we move forward, let us carry the lessons learned and the tools gained into every aspect of our lives, confident that our trials are not in vain and that our stories are part of a much larger, divine narrative.

Closing Thoughts

As we draw our study to a close, let's pause to reflect on the ground we have covered together. Over the past four weeks, we've journeyed through understanding our responses to health challenges, managing fear and anxiety, balancing rest with caregiving, and seeing our individual stories as part of a larger divine narrative. Each step has offered its challenges and its gifts, its tears and its triumphs. Today, we gather these threads, weaving them into a tapestry of faith that speaks of survival and perseverance.

You are not alone.

This refrain has echoed through each week, a constant reminder that in the midst of our trials, we are surrounded—by the presence of God, by the fellowship of believers, and by the communion of saints across time and space. We have seen that our struggles, while deeply personal, are also shared. They connect us to the heartaches and hopes of others and invite us into a community of mutual support and understanding.

A Journey Through Scripture

From the reassurances of Psalm 23 that we are led and comforted by our Shepherd, to the powerful promises in Romans 5 that suffering produces perseverance, character, and hope, Scripture has been our foundation. We've been reminded that our God is a God of all comfort, who comforts us so that we may comfort others (2 Corinthians 1:3-4). We've been encouraged to see our weaknesses as the backdrop for the display of God's strength (2 Corinthians 12:9). And we've been called to fix our eyes not on what is seen, but on what is unseen (2 Corinthians 4:18), for the eternal promises of God frame our temporary trials.

Living What We've Learned

As we conclude this study, our challenge is to carry forward the truths we've embraced into our everyday lives. It's one thing to study about faith-filled responses to health challenges; it's another to live them out when the pain is real, the fear is palpable, and the fatigue is overwhelming. How, then, can we ensure that the seeds planted here bear lasting fruit?

1. Continue in the Word: Make Scripture reading and meditation a daily habit. The truths we've explored must continually nourish our souls if they are to change our lives.

2. Cultivate Community: Keep building and leaning on your community of faith. Share your burdens and your victories, and be ready to bear the burdens of others. Our journey is not meant to be walked alone.

3. Practice Presence and Prayer: Cultivate a lifestyle of prayer where ongoing dialogue with God becomes your natural response to every situation. Let His presence infuse every moment with peace and purpose.

4. Embrace Vulnerability: Allow others to see your struggles as well as your strengths. Your vulnerability can become a bridge for others who are too weary or scared to share their own battles.

5. Seek and Offer Support: Be proactive in seeking support when you need it and offering it when you see others in need. Remember, our comfort from God is not just for us—it's meant to be shared.

A Benediction

As we part ways in this study, may you go forth with the peace of God that surpasses all understanding guarding your hearts and minds in Christ Jesus (Philippians 4:7). May you find joy in the journey, strength in the struggle, and Christ in the chaos. May your moments of despair be met with divine comfort, and may your periods of health be times of helping others.

May you remember that your story is an open letter of God's grace, read by everyone who knows you. May your life be a testament to the truth that while our bodies are fragile, our spirit can be unbreakable when anchored in Him.

And finally, may you live fully in the reality that you are not alone—not ever. The God who began a good work in you will carry it on to completion until the day of Christ Jesus (Philippians 1:6). He is the Author of your faith, the Finisher of your story, and the Keeper of your heart.

You are loved, upheld, and unshaken. Let that truth echo in every valley and from every mountaintop. Let it guide you in moments of doubt and lift you in times of praise. As you continue to face each day with its potential for pain and promise, may you do so with the unshakable conviction that you are held, you are loved, and you are ever enveloped in the grace of God.

Go in peace, live in grace, and serve with love.

Stay Connected

Thank you for joining me in *Unshaken: Faith-Filled Responses to Health Challenges*! I hope it encouraged you to find peace in your health struggle and trust God with your story. I'd love to stay connected with you as you continue to seek God in His Word. Here are a few ways to stay in touch:

Bible studies & devotionals: Unlock the Treasure of God's Word: Authored by Heather M. Dixon, whose studies have guided over 50,000 women, these workbooks are a roadmap to a deeper, more enriching faith. Whether you're a beginner or a seasoned scholar, there's a study waiting to elevate your understanding and bring you closer to God.

Available Studies by Heather:

- ‣ Ready: Finding the Courage to Face the Unknown: a six-week study of Joshua 1-5
- ‣ Determined: Living Like Jesus in Every Moment, a six-week study of Luke
- ‣ Renewed: Finding Hope When You Don't Like Your Story, a four-week study of Ruth from Naomi's perspective

No Dusty Bibles Podcast & Community: Your Go-To Online Community for Daily Bible Engagement: with Heather and Hannah as your guide, delve into just two chapters a day at a sustainable, rewarding pace. Through emails, the No Dusty Bibles podcast, our private Facebook group, and YouTube teachings, you'll never feel alone on your faith journey. We provide the resources, the community, and the daily nudges to keep you in the Word. Say goodbye to that dusty, untouched Bible and hello to a vibrant, daily walk with God.

Shoot us an email at hello@therescuedletters.com! We would love to know how we can pray for you, support you, and cheer you on.

Connect

@rescuedletters

Contact Us

hello@therescuedletters.com

Share

#rescuedletters
#unshakenstudy

Visit Us Online

www.therescuedletters.com

Listen In

No Dusty Bibles Podcast

ENDNOTES

1. The VEDS Movement. "What Is Vascular Ehlers-Danlos Syndrome? - the VEDS Movement." The VEDS Movement, 20 Jan. 2023, thevedsmovement.org/veds/what-is-veds.

2. Galatians 5:22-23

3. EKR Foundation. "Elisabeth Kübler-Ross Biography - EKR Foundation." EKR Foundation, 23 Mar. 2023, www.ekrfoundation.org/elisabeth-kubler-ross/biography

4. Rick Brannan, ed., Lexham Research Lexicon of the Greek New Testament, Lexham Research Lexicons (Bellingham, WA: Lexham Press, 2020)

5. National Alliance on Mental Illness. "Anxiety Disorders | NAMI." NAMI, 6 Mar. 2024, www.nami.org/about-mental-illness/mental-health-conditions/anxiety-disorders.

6. Strong's Concordance, s.v. Agonia, https://biblehub.com/greek/74.htm

Made in United States
Orlando, FL
15 April 2025